Peter Malin

Series Editor: Marian Co

'Tis Pity She's a Whore

John Ford

Philip Allan Updates
Market Place
Deddington
Oxfordshire
OX15 0SE

Orders

Bookpoint Ltd, 130 Milton Park, Abingdon, Oxfordshire, OX14 4SB
tel: 01235 827720
fax: 01235 400454
e-mail: uk.orders@bookpoint.co.uk
Lines are open 9.00 a.m.–5.00 p.m., Monday to Saturday, with a 24-hour message answering service. You can also order through the Philip Allan Updates website: www.philipallan.co.uk

Printed in Malta

Environmental information
Philip Allan Updates' policy is to use papers that are natural, renewable and recyclable products and made from wood grown in sustainable forests. The logging and manufacturing processes are expected to conform to the environmental regulations of the country of origin.

Contents

Introduction

Aims of the guide

The purpose of this Student Text Guide to *'Tis Pity She's a Whore* is to support your study of the play, whether you are approaching it as an examination text or for coursework. It is not a substitute for your own reading, rereading, thinking and note-making about the text. The ideas about the play contained in this guide are based on the interpretation of one reader. What the examiners want is *your own* considered response, and they can easily recognise an answer that simply repeats a critical viewpoint at second hand. As you use this guide, you should be constantly questioning what it says; you may find yourself disagreeing with some of the analysis, which in itself could form an interesting starting-point for your own interpretative view.

Quotations and line references in this guide refer to the New Mermaid text of the play edited by Martin Wiggins (2nd edition, 2003). If you are using another edition, the references should be easy enough to find, though there may be occasional slight differences, particularly in scenes containing prose. References to plays by Shakespeare are to the Oxford *Complete Works*, edited by Stanley Wells and Gary Taylor (2nd edition, Clarendon Press, 2005). In referring to modern performances of *'Tis Pity She's a Whore*, the initials RSC stand for the Royal Shakespeare Company. Dates given refer to the year in which a particular production opened.

The remainder of this *Introduction* outlines the principal exam board Assessment Objectives, and offers advice on revision and how to approach both coursework and exam essays. I am indebted to the series editor, Marian Cox, whose own Student Text Guides I have used in composing this introductory section.

The *Text Guidance* section consists of a series of chapters covering key aspects of the play. These include contexts; a scene-by-scene commentary on the play; analysis of characters, language and themes; the play's critical and theatrical afterlife; useful quotations; and a selected glossary of literary terms.

The final section, *Questions and Answers*, includes suggested essay questions, sample essay plans with marking guidelines, and two exemplar essays.

Exam board specifications

'Tis Pity She's a Whore features on a number of exam specifications for either AS or A2. It is also possible to study the play for coursework, either by itself or in comparison with another text.

It is important that you scrutinise the specification you are following. This will indicate not just where the play fits into the context of the whole subject, but such practical matters as the format and style of exam questions, how long you have to answer them, and whether you are allowed to have your copy of the text in the exam room with you. Most importantly, the specification makes clear which of the Assessment Objectives are tested through your response to this particular text, and what their relative weighting is. This is just as important if you are producing a coursework essay on the play.

Assessment Objectives

The Assessment Objectives (AOs) for AS and A2 English Literature are common to all boards:

AO1	communicate clearly the knowledge, understanding and insight appropriate to literary study, using appropriate terminology and accurate and coherent written expression
AO2i	respond with knowledge and understanding to literary texts of different types and periods
AO2ii	respond with knowledge and understanding to literary texts of different types and periods, exploring and commenting on relationships and comparisons between literary texts
AO3	show detailed understanding of the ways in which writers' choices of form, structure and language shape meanings
AO4	articulate independent opinions and judgements, informed by different interpretations of literary texts by other readers
AO5i	show understanding of the contexts in which literary texts are written and understood
AO5ii	evaluate the significance of cultural, historical and other contextual influences on literary texts and study

A summary and paraphrase of each Assessment Objective is given below and would be worth memorising:

AO1	clarity of written communication
AO2	informed personal response in relation to time and genre (literary context)
AO3	the creative literary process (context of writing)
AO4	critical and interpretative response (context of reading)
AO5	evaluation of influences (cultural context)

It is essential that you pay close attention to the AOs and their weightings for the board for which you are entered: your teacher will be able to give you this information. For example, in AQA Specification A, the dominant AO on 'Tis Pity She's a Whore is AO5i; hence you would need to concentrate on demonstrating an awareness of the contexts in which the play was written and staged as well as how later cultural changes have affected interpretations of it. Once you have identified the relevant AOs and their weightings, you must address them *explicitly* in your answer, in addition to showing your overall familiarity with and understanding of the text and demonstrating your ability to offer a clear, relevant and convincing argument.

Coursework

You will probably be able to choose your own focus for coursework, but it is vital that the topic you choose enables you to meet the relevant Assessment Objectives. For a comparative essay, you need to check if you are required to compare the play with any particular genre of text, e.g. a novel, or a play from another period. You then need to choose a text that has obvious points of comparison and contrast, for example another tragedy of love, such as Shakespeare's *Romeo and Juliet*; or another revenge tragedy, such as Middleton and Rowley's *The Changeling*; or a text that deals with difficult and controversial issues, such as Ian McEwan's novel, *The Cement Garden*, which also features an incestuous relationship.

You may be allowed to present a creative response to the text as your coursework assignment. This should be accompanied by an explanation of the rationale behind your approach and an account of how it relates to the text.

Although handwritten essays may be permissible, it is far better to word process your coursework. Not only will this make your own process of composition and redrafting easier, but it also shows consideration for your teachers and for coursework moderators, who have a large number of lengthy essays to read and assess. Double line spacing will help them to annotate your work.

From the moment you begin planning your essay, you need to be aware of how long it is expected to be. Essays that diverge radically from the word limit, in either direction, are penalised. Again, using a computer enables you to keep a regular check on the number of words you have written.

Approaching a coursework essay

You should be given a reasonable period of time to produce your essay. Don't assume that this means you can relax. If you have 3 weeks to complete your essay, don't leave it until the middle of the third week before you begin. After all, if you were writing a 45-minute exam essay, you would not sit doing nothing for the first 35 minutes. There are a number of key stages in the coursework writing process:

- Choose your title and discuss it with your teacher as soon as possible.
- Make sure you know what the examiners expect from a coursework essay for the specification you are following. Always focus on the Assessment Objectives that are actually being tested through the coursework unit — ask your teacher to make sure.
- Reread the play and all the notes and essays you have already written on it, extract what is relevant and start to allow ideas to develop in your mind.
- Set aside an hour to jot down ideas for the essay and convert them into an essay plan. Share this plan with your teacher and make use of any feedback offered.
- Identify any background reading, such as textual criticism, that may be useful to you, gather the books you need, read them and make notes.
- Give yourself a reasonable period to draft the essay, working with your text, your notes and other useful materials around you.
- Keep referring back to the title or question, and make sure that you remain focused on it.
- Allow time for your teacher to read and comment on at least part of your draft.
- Redraft your essay until you are satisfied with it. Keep checking that you have focused on the relevant Assessment Objectives.
- Leave plenty of time to complete your final version. Don't just copy it up from your draft — be prepared to add and edit, rephrase and polish.
- A bibliography will add to the professionalism of your essay. This should list all the texts you have quoted from and consulted. Check with your teacher whether you are required to use any particular format for a bibliography, and do not deviate from it.
- Proofread your essay carefully before handing it in.

Examinations

Revision advice

For the examined units it is possible that either brief or extensive revision will be necessary because the original study of the text took place some time previously. It is therefore useful to know how to go about revising and which tried and tested methods are considered the most successful for literature exams at all levels, from GCSE to degree finals. There are no short-cuts to effective exam revision; the only way to know a text well, and to know your way around it in an exam, is to have done the necessary studying. If you use the following method for both open and closed book revision, you will not only revisit and reassess all your previous work on the text in a manageable way but will be able to distil, organise and retain your knowledge. Don't try to do it all in one go: take regular breaks for refreshment and a change of scene.

(1) Between a month and a fortnight before the exam, depending on your schedule (a simple list of stages with dates displayed in your room, not a work of art), you

will need to reread the text, this time taking stock of all the underlinings and marginal annotations as well. As you read, collect onto sheets of A4 the essential ideas and quotations as you come across them. The acts of selecting key material and recording it as notes are natural ways of stimulating thought and aiding memory.

(2) Reread the highlighted areas and marginal annotations in your critical extracts and background handouts, and add anything useful from them to your list of notes and quotations. Then reread your previous essays and the teachers' comments. As you look back through essays written earlier in the course, you should have the pleasant sensation of realising that you can now write much better on the text than you could then. You will also discover that much of your huge file of notes is redundant or repeated, and that you have changed your mind about some beliefs, so that the distillation process is not too daunting. Selecting what is important is the way to crystallise your knowledge and understanding.

(3) During the run-up to the exam you need to do lots of practice essay plans to help you identify any gaps in your knowledge and give you practice in planning in 5–8 minutes. A range of titles for you to plan is provided in this guide, some of which can be done as full timed essays — and marked strictly according to exam criteria — which will show whether length and timing are problematic for you. If you have not seen a copy of a real exam paper before you take your first module, ask to see a past paper so that you are familiar with the layout and rubric.

(4) About a week before the exam, reduce your two or three sides of A4 notes to a double-sided postcard of very small dense writing. Collect a group of key words by once again selecting and condensing, and use abbreviations for quotations (first and last word), and character and place names (initials). The act of choosing and writing out the short quotations will help you to focus on the essential issues, and to recall them quickly in the exam. Make sure that your selection covers the main themes and includes examples of symbolism, style, comments on character, examples of irony, point of view or other significant aspects of the text. Previous class discussion and essay writing will have indicated which quotations are useful for almost any title; pick those which can serve more than one purpose, for instance those which reveal character and theme, and are also an example of language. In this way a minimum number of quotations can have maximum application.

(5) You now have in a compact, accessible form all the material for any possible essay title. There are only half a dozen themes relevant to a literary text so if you have covered these you should not meet with any nasty surprises when you read the exam questions. You do not need to refer to your file of paperwork again, or even to the text. For the few days before the exam, you can read through your handy postcard whenever and wherever you get the opportunity. Each time you read it, which will only take a few minutes, you will be reminding yourself of all the information you

will be able to recall in the exam to adapt to the general title or to support an analysis of particular passages.

(6) A fresh, active mind works wonders, and information needs time to settle, so don't try to cram just before the exam. Relax the night before and get a good night's sleep. In this way you will be able to enter the exam room feeling the confidence of the well-prepared candidate.

Approaching an exam essay

Your precise approach to writing an essay in exam conditions will depend on how long you have to write it, the Assessment Objectives that are being tested, and whether you are allowed to have your copy of the text with you in the exam.

Choosing a question

- Choose carefully from any options available.
- The apparently 'easier' choice will not necessarily show you at your best: you might be tempted just to reproduce stale ideas without much thought.
- A question that looks more challenging may well result in much greater engagement with the issues and argument as you write.
- However, you must choose a question that you can approach with confidence.

Planning

- Identify and highlight the key words in the question. As you write the essay, keep checking back to ensure that you are dealing with these.
- If the question requires you to focus on a particular passage, either in your own text or printed on the exam paper, read through the passage, making brief annotations as you do so. You should know the text well enough not to be baffled by anything the set section contains.
- Brainstorm your ideas on your answer sheet. This should take no more than 3 or 4 minutes.
- Plan your essay. You will not have time to create a formal and detailed plan, but you should at least highlight on your brainstormed notes a rational order in which to deal with the points you have identified.
- If the question is in parts, either implicitly or explicitly, make sure you give equal attention to each separate requirement.
- Jot down the characters, themes, scenes, speeches, images etc. that might be useful in each part of your essay.

Writing

- Write your introductory paragraph. This might briefly set the context, define the question's key words, and give some indication of your line of approach.

Sometimes, though, it is better to plunge straight into your analysis without any introductory waffling.

- Keep your mind partly on the quality of your own writing: think about sentence structures, paragraphing, vocabulary choices and use of appropriate technical terms. Remember those words and phrases for moving on to a new point or changing direction: 'However', 'On the other hand', 'Alternatively', 'Nevertheless', 'Even so', 'In addition' etc. These can be useful paragraph starters.
- Write the rest of the essay. Keep checking back to the key words and cross off each point on your notes/plan as you have dealt with it. Check the time at regular intervals.
- Incorporate short, relevant quotations into your argument, weaving them into the grammatical structure of your own sentences. Make the point of longer quotations clear — don't expect them to speak for themselves.
- Create a brief concluding paragraph that gives an overview of your argument without simply repeating or summarising the points you have made. Your conclusion should sound conclusive even if it does not strongly support a particular interpretation.
- Check through what you have written, looking at both content and accuracy, and make neat corrections where necessary. You may wish to add brief points, using omission marks or asterisks, but don't be tempted to make any major changes.
- Cross out your notes and planning with a neat diagonal line.

Further points

The exam paper is designed to test your ability to structure an argument around the specific issues in a question. You must not simply use the question as a peg on which to hang an essay you are determined to write. If a question or title crops up that you have tackled before, don't just regurgitate your previous essay, but try to think about the issues from a fresh perspective.

Essay questions are usually open ended. Don't assume that you are expected to find a 'right answer'; instead, you need to demonstrate the ability to look at the issue from various angles, and perhaps to reach a qualified conclusion. You should certainly not offer a dismissive, extreme or entirely one-sided response. If you do have strong views of your own, and can argue them convincingly, this is evidence of an informed personal response, but you still need to show an awareness of alternative interpretations. You will learn a great deal about what the examiners are looking for by studying:

- the published details of the subject specification
- the Assessment Objectives being tested in each particular part of the exam
- past exam papers
- the examiners' reports on the previous year's exams

Ask your teacher to go through the relevant parts of these documents with you.

Text Guidance

LITERATURE

Contexts

Historical and cultural context

A note on terminology

The reign of Queen Elizabeth I is familiarly referred to as the Elizabethan period. The equivalent adjectives referring to the reigns of her two successors derive from the Latin versions of their names, Jacobus and Carolus; thus, the reign of James I is referred to as the Jacobean period, and the reign of Charles I as the Caroline period. These terms are used frequently throughout this guide.

Politics and religion

Apart from a brief return to Catholicism under Mary I, England had been a Protestant country since Henry VIII's break with the Roman Catholic Church in the 1530s. Protestant orthodoxy represented Catholics as ritualistic idol-worshippers, politically and morally corrupt. Anti-Catholic prejudice was enshrined in the law, with draconian punishments available for varying degrees of recusancy (the refusal to embrace Protestant doctrine). England had been at war with Catholic states such as Spain, whose Armada had been triumphantly defeated in 1588, while conspiracies such as the 1605 Gunpowder Plot reinforced suspicion of the adherents of Catholicism.

Despite this, in the early 1620s, James I planned to marry his son, Charles, to a Spanish princess, arousing considerable national unease. In the event, a romantic escapade to Madrid to woo her by the disguised Prince Charles and the Duke of Buckingham proved to be an embarrassing fiasco, to the general relief of English Protestants. However, on his accession to the throne in 1625, Charles married another Catholic princess, the 15-year-old Henrietta Maria, sister of the French king. Parliament was dismayed, though its fear that Charles I himself would convert to Catholicism proved unfounded. Wars with Spain and France followed, and it must have seemed that Catholic countries could still safely be classified as 'the enemy'. Dramatists of the time frequently chose Spain and Italy as the settings for plays that demonstrated political, religious and moral corruption, and John Ford was no exception. 'Tis Pity She's a Whore is set in Parma and presents a corrupt Cardinal at the summit of its social hierarchy, his hypocritical wielding of power implicitly sanctioned by the Pope himself.

However, high-church Anglican practices, promoted particularly by William Laud, the Bishop of London and later Archbishop of Canterbury, were viewed by many traditional Protestants as veering towards Catholicism, and the Puritans were particularly vehement in their objections. Puritanism was an especially strict form of Protestantism, with its insistence on more rigid Sabbath observance and its demands for stronger measures against immorality, embodied partly in its anti-theatricalism. Theatres and other places of popular entertainment were branded by the Puritans as dens of vice which should be closed down; in some ways they had a point, since pickpockets and prostitutes, among others, plied their trade in London's theatre districts south of the Thames among the audiences thronging to the public playhouses.

Though Puritanism was at the opposite religious extreme to Catholicism, its adherents, too, inevitably found themselves attacked and pilloried in Jacobean and Caroline drama. Eventually, the Puritans were instrumental in the downfall of the monarchy, and the theatres were indeed closed down, for a variety of social, political and moral reasons, on the outbreak of the Civil War in 1642. These days, we tend to believe that religion and politics do not mix, but in the seventeenth century they were inseparable.

Women in society

Despite the example of Queen Elizabeth I, early seventeenth-century society remained firmly patriarchal and misogynistic. Women's choices were almost entirely circumscribed by men, the power exerted by their fathers being taken over on marriage by their husbands. In *'Tis Pity*, we see Annabella exposed to the marriage market, and although her father, Florio, is more benign than other fathers in Renaissance drama, insisting that he 'will not force [his] daughter 'gainst her will' (I.3.3), and wishes her not to 'marry wealth, but love' (I.3.11), she is still merely the object of a series of negotiations — partly financial — in which her choices are extremely limited. The possessiveness of her brother and lover, Giovanni, and her eventual husband, Soranzo, inflicts various forms of violence on her, and the play's other women are also ultimately the victims of male power.

Independent women like Hippolita were regarded as a threat to the social fabric, and those who, like her, did not display traditional feminine virtues — modesty, chastity, obedience, mildness — ran the risk of public humiliation or worse. Women were regarded as weak, not merely physically but in their lack of self-control. This belief fed the kind of sexual anxiety often displayed by male characters in plays of the time, as if women were sexually promiscuous almost by definition. As Soranzo puts it: 'My reason tells me now that 'tis as common / To err in frailty as to be a woman' (IV.3.144–45). On the face of it, Ford's portrayal seems to support such a view, in Hippolita's unfaithfulness to Richardetto, Annabella's transgressive sexuality and Putana's bawdy innuendo. However, these characters are not explicitly attacked in the play, and the portrayal of the patriarchal power that limits their choices is implicitly seen as sufficient reason to view their behaviour sympathetically. Even Philotis, who demonstrates all the qualities of virtuous femininity, is consigned by her uncle to life in a nunnery — supposedly for her own safety, sent away from both the dangers and temptations of the world.

One tiny textual moment will perhaps serve to illustrate how Ford exposes patriarchal assumptions in the play. Kneeling to exchange ritual vows of faithfulness, Giovanni and Annabella use the same words to express their union in love and, potentially, death, with Giovanni merely changing 'brother' to 'sister'. However, where Annabella swears 'by our mother's dust', Giovanni swears 'by my mother's dust' (I.2.248–52), a significant change that appropriates ownership of their mother to himself, the male child. Such linguistic subtleties speak volumes.

King and parliament

John Ford lived in troubled times. Although, as far as we know, he died before the outbreak of civil war in 1642, the increasing tensions in society and the potential for its violent fracture must have been as evident to him as to other intelligent observers during the late 1620s and early 1630s.

Charles I had been brought up to believe in his divine right to rule the country, and he was less amenable than other monarchs to what he saw as the interference of parliament in his management of the state. The early years of his reign were marked by a series of bitter disputes between the king and his parliament, which was dismissed and recalled on a number of occasions. Sources of conflict ranged from the incompetence of Charles's friend and supporter, the Duke of Buckingham, whose military mismanagement of the wars against France and Spain was deeply resented, to the king's attempts to extort money out of his citizens by forced loans and the revival of punitive taxes.

In 1628, Charles was forced to accede to the Petition of Right proposed by parliament, and the assassination of Buckingham — though personally rather than politically motivated — deprived him of one of his chief props. Further friction was caused by the pseudo-Catholic practices espoused by high church ministers such as Bishop Laud, and in a dramatic episode in the House of Commons, parliament passed the Three Resolutions, demanding adherence to Protestant principles, an end to Catholic influence and the outlawing of royal revenue-raising without parliamentary approval. Charles responded by dissolving parliament in 1629, instigating a period of Personal Rule that lasted for over 10 years. He imposed his will partly through the Star Chamber and the Court of High Commission. Among other things, these enabled the king's ministers to summon and punish any of his subjects without recourse to the normal legal safeguards, and to punish all 'religious' offences such as spoken or printed criticism of bishops and high church practices.

This was the context in which *'Tis Pity She's a Whore* was written and performed and, on the face of it, the play seems remote from the political turmoil that surrounded it. However, it could be argued that, under the guise of its ostensibly Italian setting, Ford is examining the consequences of a corrupt hierarchy ruling on the basis of social inequality, patriarchal power and religious hypocrisy. Shocking as it is, the incest at the centre of the play is treated with openness and a degree of sympathy, despite the conventional moralising of the Friar. Annabella is presented as a heroine worthy of tragic status, in the face of the Cardinal's contemptuous dismissal of her; and the disruption of three formal banquets during the course of the play could be seen as a symbol of the potential fracture inevitably generated by divisive social and moral structures. Viewed in this way, the play offers a subtle critique of the political status quo under Charles I and perhaps even an ominous foreshadowing of the ultimate social fracture of civil war.

During the 1630s, Charles I was increasingly faced with political problems both at home and abroad. Formal opposition to his rule grew; his abortive attempts to reinstate parliament in order to bully it into submission were dismal failures; rioting broke out in London; Laud was impeached and imprisoned; and the Earl of Strafford, the king's leading general, was executed after almost being convicted of treason. Military hostilities broke out in 1642 between the royalists or 'cavaliers' and Oliver Cromwell's 'roundheads', the pro-parliamentarians strongly supported by leading Puritans. Though Charles I was not executed until 1649, his reign was effectively over, and the monarchy remained in abeyance until its restoration under his son, Charles II, in 1660. The playwrights of the Caroline age, like Ford, could hardly avoid reflecting the turbulent times in which they lived in the theatrical dramas they produced.

Jacobean and Caroline theatre

We tend to think of early seventeenth-century theatre in terms of its most famous playhouse, the Globe, built by Shakespeare's company, the Lord Chamberlain's Men (later the King's Men), on the south bank of the Thames at Southwark in 1599. You may have been to the new Globe, an attempted reconstruction of the Elizabethan original, in London; or you may have gained an impression of such a typical open-air amphitheatre from the vivid re-creations in films such as Laurence Olivier's *Henry V* (1944) or John Madden's *Shakespeare in Love* (1998). These theatres held 2,000–3,000 spectators, and performances were given during the afternoon, illuminated by natural light. The stage was a raised wooden platform thrust into the yard or pit where spectators stood; others would pay more to view from a gallery. Scenery was minimal, with the bare stage, its canopy, rear doors and alcove, and raised balcony providing the permanent setting. Costumes were often elaborate, reflecting character and status rather than the period in which the play was set. Music and special effects added to the atmosphere, and audiences comprised members of all social groups. Also, crucially, all the parts were played by male actors, with boys playing the principal female roles, since the cultural and moral climate of the time forbade public performances by women.

However, the theatrical climate had shifted by the time Ford was writing for the theatre in the 1620s and 1630s. Although the main open-air playhouses — the

Globe, the Hope, the Rose and the Swan — were still operational, it was the indoor theatres, more expensive and more elite, that were now at the forefront of theatrical taste. They had existed since Elizabethan times, often housing children's acting companies, but it was the acquisition of the Blackfriars Theatre in 1609 by the King's Men that had a decisive effect on the ethos of playgoing. In 1625, when Charles I acceded to the throne, the Blackfriars had been joined by the Cockpit and the Salisbury Court theatres, among others. Command performances at the royal palaces also remained regular features in the calendars of the leading theatre companies, and the fashion for elaborate court masques was reflected in conventional plays too; Hippolita's ill-fated masque at Soranzo and Annabella's wedding feast is one of many examples in the drama of the time.

'Tis Pity She's a Whore was first performed at the Cockpit, also known as the Phoenix Theatre, around 1630. Like all indoor theatres, it was lit by candles, necessitating regular breaks to trim them of excess wax and perhaps substitute fresh ones. This partly explains the five-act structuring of plays, with the breaks between acts accompanied by music. The theatre's resident company was Queen Henrietta's Men, and one can imagine that the young French queen was a keen and active patron. She herself organised and acted in court performances of plays and masques, including texts by French writers such as Racine. In 1629, controversially, she hosted a visit by a French acting troupe including female performers, which played at the Blackfriars as well as at court. This must have created something of a stir in the all-male acting community of the English theatre. However, politics and theatre, like politics and religion, were inseparable, and Queen Henrietta Maria found herself attacked for her involvement in further court theatricals in 1633. William Prynne, whose criticism of her formed part of his *Histriomastix*, was arrested and tortured for his presumption.

With the Catholic queen as patron of the producing company, it may seem odd for Ford to have presented an apparently anti-Catholic bias in *'Tis Pity*, essentially through his portrayal of the Cardinal. However, it is wrong to think that Caroline dramatists were, of necessity, royalist propagandists, reflecting a morally decadent court and offering escapist fare that failed to connect with contemporary issues. Like his fellow Caroline playwrights John Fletcher, Ben Jonson, Philip Massinger, James Shirley and Richard Brome, Ford engages specifically with the political and social realities of his time; often, however, these are approached in indirect and subtle ways, distanced by foreign locations or historical contexts.

As well as being set in Italy, *'Tis Pity* is also, quite deliberately, set in the recent past — something it is now difficult for us to realise. A number of small details — the reference to 'the wars against the Milanese' (I.2.77), which took place in the 1500s; the wearing of codpieces; the absence of firearms — remove the play from too close an identification with Caroline society, but perceptive spectators would have been well aware of its contemporary resonances. Dramatists had been doing this for decades; when Shakespeare wrote about the reign of Richard II, his audiences were expected to reflect on that of Elizabeth I, as she herself was only too well aware. Like other playwrights, Ford trod a delicate and dangerous line between the patronage and the disapproval of the establishment.

John Ford's life and works

The life of John Ford spans the reigns of three monarchs: Elizabeth I, James I and Charles I. He was born in 1586, the second son of a prosperous Devon gentleman of Ilsington, on the edge of Dartmoor. He was almost certainly not the John Ford admitted to Exeter College, Oxford, in 1601, but in 1602, the final year of Queen Elizabeth's reign, he entered London's Middle Temple. This was nominally the institution where lawyers were trained, but it was also a kind of fashionable gentlemen's club, where useful contacts could be forged and cultural life enjoyed. Poets and dramatists flourished there and, as long as bills were paid and rules adhered to, it was possible to remain a member for life even if, like Ford, one was not called to the Bar. Finances do not seem to have been entirely healthy: from 1606–08 he was suspended for non-payment of his buttery bill, and his father left him a mere £10 on his death in 1610. In 1617 he may have been involved in a protest against the compulsory wearing of caps at meals and in church but, again, this was more likely to have been another John Ford.

Ford's writing career began in about 1606 with a poem entitled *Fame's Memorial*, an elegy on the death of the Earl of Devonshire. For ten years or so he wrote mostly poems and pamphlets, before turning to the theatre in about 1620 with a series of collaborative plays, not all of which have survived. During the 1620s he worked with the more experienced playwrights Thomas Dekker, William Rowley and John Webster, on plays such as *The Witch of Edmonton*, *The Spanish Gipsy*, *The Welsh Ambassador*, *The Sun's Darling*, *The Fairy Knight*, *The Bristol Merchant* and *A Late Murder of the Son upon the Mother*. He also collaborated with John Fletcher and Philip Massinger, Shakespeare's successors as chief dramatists with the King's Men, on *The Laws of Candy* and *The Fair Maid of the Inn*. His earliest independent plays, from the late 1620s (now in the reign of Charles I), were also performed by the King's Men; these were the romantic comedy *The Lover's Melancholy* and the tragedy *The Broken Heart*. In the 1630s, he worked mainly for Queen Henrietta's Men at the Phoenix Theatre, producing the tragedies *'Tis Pity She's a Whore* and *Love's Sacrifice*; the history play *Perkin Warbeck*, set in the reign of Henry VII; and the comedies *The Fancies Chaste and Noble* and *The Lady's Trial*. He also wrote occasional commendatory verses for the publication of plays by other writers, such as Webster's *The Duchess of Malfi*.

We have no idea what kind of a character Ford might have been. In 1632, William Heminges wrote of him:

> Deep in a dump Jack Ford alone was got,
> With folded arms and melancholy hat.

This, however, could merely have been an acknowledgement of Ford's interest in the melancholy personality type, explored in Robert Burton's highly influential *The Anatomy of Melancholy* (1621) and reflected in Ford's play *The Lover's Melancholy*. Nothing is recorded of Ford after 1639. Perhaps he retired to Devon prior to the outbreak of the Civil War. We do not know when he died.

Revenge tragedy

Tragedy as a dramatic form dates back to the theatre of ancient Greece. Centred on characters of high social status who suffer calamity as a result of some personal flaw, error of judgement, ignorance of the truth or divine influence, tragedy shows its protagonists achieving dignity and self-knowledge through the suffering they endure. The Greek writer Aristotle (384–322 BC) theorised about the nature of tragedy in his *Poetics*, specifying its effect on the audience as the evocation of pity and fear, emotions which are then purged and purified through what he called catharsis. English Renaissance writers were familiar with Aristotle's theories and inevitably developed their own versions of the tragic genre as theatres and plays became more sophisticated. They diverged from Aristotle particularly in notions of dramatic structure. Aristotle's concept of the unities — 'rules' specifying that a play's action should consist of one unified plot, enacted in one location and taking place within a single day — were consistently flouted. English Renaissance tragedy frequently developed subplots and comic elements, and its action was often temporally and geographically diverse.

One variant, developed by a number of writers during the last 20 years of the sixteenth century, towards the end of Elizabeth I's reign, has come to be known as revenge tragedy. Early examples, which gained great popularity, were Kyd's *The Spanish Tragedy* (1587), Marlowe's *The Jew of Malta* (1589) and Shakespeare's *Titus Andronicus* (1591).

Revenge tragedy remained popular during the first decade of the seventeenth century, under James I. Examples include Shakespeare's *Hamlet* (1600), Middleton's *The Revenger's Tragedy* (1606) and Tourneur's *The Atheist's Tragedy* (1611). Marston's *The Malcontent* (1603) was a form of revenge tragicomedy.

Like all genre classification, the term 'revenge tragedy' covers a variety of diverse plays. However, it is possible to identify some of the key features of the genre, which are listed below:

- characters whose actions are motivated by codes of honour and the desire for revenge
- bloody and violent acts, torture and madness
- elements of the supernatural, including the appearance of ghosts
- settings in foreign countries, frequently Spain or Italy
- an atmosphere of political, moral and religious corruption
- key character types, such as the malcontent and the machiavel
- a mingling of gruesome acts and tragic events with a kind of grotesque comedy
- the sense that the revenger himself is morally corrupted by the very act of revenge

The greatest revenge plays of the early seventeenth century transcend the apparently restricting confines of the genre, offering complex and ambiguous reflections on the nature of revenge and its impact on both its practitioners and its victims. *The Spanish Tragedy* remained a popular theatrical model, but it was parodied as much as it was admired. Its portentous dramatic machinery of ghosts and dumb shows, elaborate rhetoric, assumed madness and theatrical self-awareness was reinvented as part of a more sophisticated approach to the telling of stories of revenge. In *Hamlet*, for example, the visceral, emotional impact of the urge for revenge is replaced by an intellectual, philosophical tone appropriate to a revenger who thinks so much that his revenge is repeatedly deferred as he questions the entire meaning of existence. In other plays, revenge becomes merely one among many motives in the drama, and the revenger is not necessarily the central focus. Many critics therefore consider 'revenge tragedy' to be an unhelpful classification, preferring 'tragedy of blood' as a more appropriate generic term.

Revenge tragedy retained its appeal throughout the Jacobean period and into the Caroline age, and Ford owed a particular debt to the great dramas of John Webster and Thomas Middleton, which represent complex examples of the genre. In Webster's *The White Devil*, the lovers Bracciano and Vittoria, aided by Vittoria's brother Flamineo, contrive the murder of their respective spouses. Brought to trial for murder and adultery, however, Vittoria is presented as the noble victim of a corrupt society, and the subsequent complications of revenge and counter-revenge elicit conflicting and ambivalent responses from the audience. In *The Duchess of Malfi*, too, Webster portrays multiple acts of revenge. Ferdinand and the Cardinal viciously revenge themselves on their sister, merely because she has remarried in opposition to their wishes. Their chief instrument, Bosola, then turns against them to revenge the murder of the Duchess, which he himself was instrumental in committing.

In *Women Beware Women*, Middleton weaves a complex web of intrigue and revenge, presided over by the cynically manipulative Livia and culminating in multiple murders enacted during a celebratory masque. In *The Changeling*, written by Middleton in collaboration with William Rowley, a young bride, Beatrice-Joanna, employs her hated servant, De Flores, to murder her unwanted suitor, but the murderer demands her sexual favours as his reward, thus polluting her subsequent marriage to Alsemero, the man she loves. The passion and vengeance of the main plot are set against scenes in a madhouse, suggesting a world in terminal moral and emotional disintegration.

Ford's own first attempt at tragedy, *The Broken Heart*, is cooler and less obviously extravagant in its dissection of the revengeful consequences of an enforced marriage. Nevertheless, it manages to incorporate many of the standard motifs of the revenge genre, and devises a striking series of deaths for its four principal characters: Penthea dies quietly after declining into madness; Ithocles is stabbed after being trapped in a trick chair; Orgilus is bled to death on stage; and Calantha carefully orchestrates the moment of her own death of a broken heart.

Many of the features of revenge tragedy are present, too, in *'Tis Pity She's a Whore*, where the number of revengers gradually increases during the play, including Grimaldi, Richardetto, Hippolita and Soranzo. The play's treatment of the theme of revenge is dealt with on pages 71–73 of this guide.

Sources of the play

The term 'sources' is perhaps a misleading one. It suggests that a writer creates a literary or dramatic work while surrounded by a variety of other texts, reshaping plots, characters, ideas and language into something new and distinctive. Sometimes this is undoubtedly true, but sources often work in a less organised, more amorphous way, taking in memories and recollections, personal experience, contemporary cultural preoccupations and current events, in addition to the more specific influence of other plays, stories, poems and historical accounts.

While many plays of the period are closely based on one or more particular source, Ford seems merely to have developed a few aspects of his narrative, as well as one or two of the character names, from a variety of texts including John Florio's *First Fruits*, George Whetstone's *Heptameron of Civil Discourses* and François Rosset's *Histoires Tragiques de Notre Temps*, which deals with an incestuous relation-ship between a student and his sister. None of these are significant enough to throw much light on Ford's play. One source text, however, offers revealing insights into Ford's purposes.

'Tis Pity She's a Whore and *Romeo and Juliet*

It is clear that in many aspects of *'Tis Pity*, Ford is deliberately echoing Shakespeare's tragedy of young love, written over 30 years previously. Annabella, like Juliet, is a young girl whose father is concerned with arranging an advantageous marriage for her. Ford increases the tension by facing her with three suitors, Grimaldi, Bergetto and Soranzo, rather than the one, Count Paris, whom Capulet has in mind for Juliet. Though Annabella is motherless, unlike Juliet, she does have a nurse, Putana, who fulfils much the same role as Juliet's Nurse. Both characters are jolly, earthy and bawdy, with a knowing attitude to sex, but in Putana these characteristics are much less appealing. Both characters encourage their charges in their ill-advised relationships, and both ultimately let them down — Juliet's Nurse by advising her to marry Paris, and Putana by revealing to Vasques the identity of Annabella's lover. While Juliet's Nurse merely fades out of the final section of the play, Putana suffers a terrible punishment for her complicity in illicit love, reflecting the much darker tone of Ford's play.

Like Romeo, Giovanni has an alternative father-figure in the Friar. While the friars of both plays obviously have enormous affection for their young protégés, Bonaventura never encourages Giovanni's relationship with Annabella though, like Friar Lawrence, he interferes to the extent of urging and celebrating a marriage he considers morally appropriate. Just as Friar Lawrence abandons Juliet when things go wrong — 'I dare no longer stay' (*Romeo and Juliet*, V.3.159) — so Bonaventura ultimately abdicates responsibility: 'I must not stay' (V.3.65). Outside his relationship with the Friar, Giovanni is a lonely character, revelling in melancholy reflections, in contrast to Romeo who, despite his withdrawn and melancholy state at the beginning of the play, is essentially sociable, with a large group of friends. The lovers in both plays, of course, are faced with an apparently insuperable barrier to their relationship: in *Romeo and Juliet* it is a merely social barrier, in the form of the violent feud between Montagues and Capulets; in *'Tis Pity* it is the fact that they are brother and sister — a moral impediment which runs the risk of alienating the audience.

There are other parallels between the two plays that are worth exploring. Bergetto, for example, occupies a similar dramatic role to Mercutio: both are responsible for creating comedy in the first half of each play, and both meet violent and mistaken deaths halfway through. Where Bergetto is terminally stupid, however, his role entirely in prose, Mercutio is supremely witty and intelligent, his questing spirit often finding expression in brilliant flights of verse. The Cardinal and the Prince also occupy parallel roles. Both are authority figures who are called on to dispense judgement following one or more violent deaths halfway through each play, as well as at the tragic climaxes, each of them being given their play's concluding words. As so often, though, Ford twists the perspective of Shakespeare's drama, turning the moral authority of Prince Escalus into the cynical hypocrisy of the Cardinal. It seems that Ford is both paying homage to Shakespeare's play and using it as the springboard to create something edgier and more shocking.

The printed text

The earliest printed edition of *'Tis Pity She's a Whore* was the Quarto of 1633. This probably used Ford's own manuscript as the basis of the text. Despite some inevitable printing errors, this first published edition seems reasonably accurate, and there is no reason to think that it differs markedly from the version performed at the Phoenix Theatre and elsewhere.

Your modern edition of the play will differ from the original Quarto in a number of respects. Where there are problems — in knowing, for example, whether some lines should be printed as prose or verse — different modern editors make different decisions. Consequently, you will find slight but sometimes significant differences between modern editions of the play. Some of the principal changes made by modern editors are as follows:

- Correcting obvious misprints.
- Altering spelling and punctuation to conform to modern conventions.
- Identifying apparent errors and difficulties in the Quarto text and attempting to provide a reading that makes sense.
- Rationalising stage directions to give a clearer idea of the action.
- Adding line numbers to each scene; these may be different in different editions because lines of prose occupy varying amounts of space depending on the format of the edition and the typeface used.

Many of these editorial practices, however, are acts of interpretation as much as clarification, and can have a variety of problematic effects:

- Changing the way a sentence is punctuated can alter its meaning, shift its emphasis or remove deliberate ambiguities.
- Modernising spelling can obscure the Caroline pronunciation, perhaps eliminating subtle effects of assonance or onomatopoeia.
- Fixing stage directions can limit a reader's awareness of alternative ways of staging a scene.

Here are a few small examples of editorial variants, so that you can make up your own mind how important they are.

At I.3.29, the Quarto gives the line, 'How now, Bergetto, whither away so fast?' to Poggio. Most editors, such as Derek Roper in the Revels Student edition, give it instead to Donado, which seems more appropriate in context. Martin Wiggins, however, assigns it to Poggio in his New Mermaids edition, justifying his decision in a footnote. Similarly, the Quarto gives the line, 'There's hope of this yet' at III.5.37 to Philotis. Again, Wiggins sticks to this, but Simon Barker in his Routledge edition gives it to Poggio and earlier editors have given it to Richardetto. It is worth considering why you think editors have felt the need to change the

Quarto text on these two occasions, and what you think would seem most logical and effective in performing the play.

Two words will suffice to show how editors disagree even on spelling. Martin Wiggins has the Friar credit Giovanni with a fine reputation throughout 'Bologna' (I.1.49), while Poggio later refers to Bergetto's love of 'parmesan' (I.3.59). Derek Roper, however, sticks to the Quarto's spellings of 'Bononia' and 'parmasent', making the text seem much more archaic to a modern reader. Again, it is worth considering what you would have actors say in a production.

As these examples show, you should get into the habit of using your edition critically and questioning its assumptions. If you think of the text as a blueprint for a theatrical performance, with all the staging alternatives that this implies, you cannot go far wrong.

Scene summaries and commentary

As with all parts of this guide, you should use this section critically. It is not a substitute for your own close reading of the text: there are other angles and inter-pretations that are not considered here. Question everything you read and weigh it against your own understanding of each scene. The commentary in particular is highly selective. It cannot cover every aspect of every scene, and the focus here is usually on character, with regular reflections on themes, language and staging possibilities.

Act I scene 1

Giovanni is arguing passionately with Friar Bonaventura, to whom he has confessed his love for his sister, Annabella. The Friar urges on him repentance for his incestuous lust, to avoid the consequence of eternal damnation. Giovanni, though he attempts to justify his feelings, nevertheless seems to accept the Friar's advice.

Opening a play in mid-argument is an effective dramatic device, demanding the audience's immediate attention to the dispute in hand. Among other plays of the period that use the same technique are Shakespeare's *Othello* and Jonson's *The Alchemist*. Here, though, the shock value is much greater as it emerges that Giovanni has breached one of the strongest cultural taboos in succumbing to incestuous feelings towards his sister. Even more shocking is his attempt to justify such feelings through the kind of intellectual debating points in which he has evidently excelled at the University of Bologna. To the Friar – and, on the whole, to Ford's audience – the issue is not a matter for debate, as he makes clear in his opening speech. Rather, it is a straightforward question of sin and lust, carrying the punishment of eternal damnation, which the Friar already envisages for Giovanni, the 'wilful flames' of his lust anticipating the fires of hell.

Neither of the characters in the scene is particularly sympathetic. There is an arrogant, petulant immaturity to Giovanni's assumption that deep moral and religious issues can be subjected to the academic niceties of debating. His arguments are essentially selfish, characterising sibling relationships as a mere 'customary form, from man to man' that stands in the way of his own 'perpetual happiness'. He literally idolises his sister, claiming even 'the gods' would worship her if she were newly created. This outrages the Friar, as much for Giovanni's reference to pagan deities rather than the Christian God, as for his blasphemy in setting up his sister as an alternative object of worship. It is notable that when Giovanni apparently accepts the Friar's advice at the end of the scene, he does so not because he has been convinced of his own moral wickedness, but merely to save himself from 'the rod /Of vengeance'. Giovanni ends, again blasphemously, threatening to worship 'fate' rather than God, to which the Friar is given no reply. Throughout the scene, Giovanni shows no sense of shame for his illicit feelings, merely the self-pity of one whose desires have been thwarted.

Though Giovanni claims to see 'pity and compassion' in the Friar's eyes, to us the Friar's response is largely one of shock, outrage and condemnation. To him, rational argument is a threat to religious faith, leading down the path to 'devilish atheism'. As he says, it is better 'To bless the sun, than reason why it shines'. His language is the melodramatic discourse of the hellfire preacher, threatening Giovanni that 'death waits on [his] lust' – the 'leprosy of lust /That rots [his] soul'. With no sense of irony, he can proclaim that, in its punishment of such sins, 'Heaven is just'. It seems odd, then, that part of his advice to Giovanni encourages him to seek out other women on the grounds that, although any sexual relationship outside marriage is sinful, ''tis much less sin' than his love for his sister. The strength of the Friar's feelings can be partly attributed to a sense of severe disappointment in Giovanni, whose reputation for scholarly excellence, developed under the Friar's 'tutelage', is now compromised. Perhaps there is more, too: the Friar has evidently given up his own austere religious life to follow Giovanni to university, choosing 'Rather to leave my books than part with thee'. Ford seems to be inviting us to consider a sexual attraction on the Friar's part towards his pupil, so that his extreme reaction may incorporate an element of jealousy. For most of Ford's audience, though, Giovanni's incestuous feelings in themselves would be enough to arouse the Friar's passionate outrage.

Ford lays the groundwork for the play's imagery in this opening scene. The play partly examines the ambiguous borderlines between love and lust, and their outcome in death, and these words are prominent from the start. (It should not be forgotten that, in Ford's time, 'death' was also a metaphor for orgasm.) 'Heart' and 'blood' are also prominent in the imagery of the play as a whole, and are emphasised here. Both words carry associations of love, passion and death, and Ford builds them into a pattern that reaches appropriate completion in the play's final scene. Fate, too, set up by Giovanni as an alternative to religious faith in the scene's closing line, is another repeated motif in the linguistic structure of the play, and 'vengeance', attributed here to God, develops into a key human motive in the play's narrative.

Act I scene 2

Grimaldi, a Roman gentleman, fights with Vasques, Soranzo's Spanish servant, outside Florio's house; Vasques wins the fight. Disturbed by the altercation, Florio comes out with Soranzo and Donado. It emerges that Grimaldi and Soranzo are rivals for the love of Florio's daughter, Annabella — who observes the scene from above, with her nurse, Putana; Vasques has been defending his master's honour in the face of Grimaldi's disparaging remarks. Grimaldi leaves, swearing revenge. Florio rebukes Soranzo and Vasques, suggesting that Soranzo has already won Annabella's heart; they return indoors. Remaining on the upper level, Putana talks to Annabella about her suitors, saying she would prefer Soranzo if it weren't for his previous adulterous relationship with Hippolita, now a widow. Donado's nephew Bergetto, another of Annabella's suitors, comes out of the house with his servant, Poggio; he seems confident that Annabella will be his. They go back in and Giovanni appears, consumed with melancholy. While Annabella and Putana descend to talk to him, he admits in soliloquy that his feelings for his sister are as strong as ever. Putana is dismissed and Giovanni confesses his love for Annabella, who tells him she has felt the same way about him for some time. They exchange vows of love and faith, and go indoors to consummate their relationship sexually.

Like scene 1, this scene begins in the middle of a dispute, but its participants are engaged in physical violence rather than intellectual and theological debate. The participants are also differentiated by their use of colloquial prose, in which they exchange threats and insults, contrasted with the formal if passionate blank verse of Giovanni and the Friar. We do not learn who these characters are until their fight is cut short by the intervention of Florio and his dinner guests, but it is clear that one of them, Vasques, is a servant, contemptuously referred to by the other as 'slave' and 'cast-suit'; and the other, Grimaldi, professes to be a gentleman and a soldier, both of which claims are denied by his opponent, who calls him a 'poor shadow of a soldier' and suggests that his own master has servants of a higher standing than this so-called 'Roman [...] gentleman'. Social distinctions are crucial in the world of the play, and the consequences of impugning someone's social status are made clear here.

When Florio and the others appear, it becomes clear that Grimaldi and Soranzo are rivals for Annabella's love, and that Vasques has been defending his master's honour against Grimaldi's attempts to denigrate him to Annabella. With the appearance of Bergetto later in the scene, Annabella is established for the audience with three rival suitors, two of whom, Grimaldi and Soranzo, are noblemen of a superior social class, Florio being merely a middle-class citizen. Giovanni's love for his sister is thus seen to face more impediments than merely its incestuous nature.

However, Ford does not make us feel that any of Annabella's suitors is worthy of her. Grimaldi is hot-tempered, always stressing his social status – which may, as Soranzo admits, make him 'equal' to himself in blood yet is diminished by his 'lowness [of] mind', making him 'base' in his rival's eyes. Soranzo, for his part, is responsible for the 'sudden broils' that so upset his host and prospective father-in-law, having instructed Vasques to 'correct [Grimaldi's] tongue' on his behalf, since it would be demeaning to fight with him in person. Bergetto, meanwhile, is presented as an empty-headed 'idiot', confident that he will 'have the wench' because his uncle, Donado, says so. Interestingly, Bergetto's name is the only one not spoken in the scene, emphasising Putana's description of him as a mere 'cipher' or nonentity; a striking contrast with both Grimaldi, who is named three times in the space of 26 lines, and Poggio, whose name Bergetto uses five times in a mere 15 lines of dialogue.

Ford's decision to introduce us to Annabella as a mere observer of events rather than a participant is interesting and dramatically effective, particularly in the way all her suitors, including Giovanni, are paraded below for her (and our) examination, with a kind of running commentary by Putana. This scene has many echoes of Shakespeare's *Troilus and Cressida*, in which the heroine and her uncle, Pandarus – a character who has much in common with both Putana and the Nurse in *Romeo and Juliet* – look down on the returning Trojan warriors, commenting on each, with the genuine object of affection appearing last. Putana, like Pandarus, is a cruder, more earthy version of Juliet's Nurse, her commentary on the three suitors replete with sexual innuendo; indeed, each of them is considered by her primarily in terms of his likely sexual potency (see lines 78–82, 89–91, 123–26). Putana is Annabella's 'tut'ress', but seems hardly qualified for such a role. She, in turn, persistently addresses Annabella as her 'charge', suggesting a responsibility for her young mistress that she hardly fulfils. She is a lively, funny character, but one of dubious moral standing – though she does seem to object to Soranzo's previous illicit relationship with 'Hippolita the lusty widow in her husband's lifetime'. This passing reference is something we need to remember.

Our first impression of Annabella will be gained from her response to what she observes from the upper level. The actor of the role has a number of options: is she amused or annoyed? Irritated or indifferent? When she speaks, she seems discontented and melancholy, claiming to find no pleasure in being the object of rival suitors and expressing irritation with Putana's bawdy chatter, suggesting she has been at the bottle (see line 99). Bergetto is the only suitor on whom she ventures an opinion: 'This idiot haunts me too'.

The scene dramatically changes gear on Giovanni's entrance. Up to this point, the dialogue has been mostly in prose, with the intervention of Florio and the others in verse; indeed, Vasques, Putana, Bergetto and Poggio are prose characters throughout the play. Now, however, the scene is lifted almost wholly into the blank verse appropriate to a passionate soliloquy and romantic encounter, though Ford cleverly marks the initial awkwardness and uncertainty of the lovers' discourse with dialogue that could be either prose or rough and irregular verse (see in particular lines 162–68, 175–86).

The scene between them moves through various clearly defined stages. First, Annabella reflects on Giovanni's attractiveness and his evident sorrow. Then, while she and Putana descend, Giovanni bewails his 'ruin', having tried and failed to conquer his illicit love, and determines to tell her how he feels. Having got rid of Putana, Giovanni then builds awkwardly to a confession of his love; in turn, Annabella reveals that she has long felt the same way about him. Finally, having knelt to exchange vows and kisses in a sort of wedding parody, they head off to bed to consummate their relationship. Ford's writing in this sequence is rich and eloquent, and the emotional depth with which he explores the lovers' feelings indicates, I think, that he intends to evoke the audience's sympathy and approval in the face of their natural revulsion from the sin of incest. Of the two, Giovanni is perhaps less sympathetic, resorting to an outright lie in claiming to Annabella 'I have asked counsel of the holy Church, / Who tells me I may love you'. There is little sense in this love scene, however, that Giovanni and Annabella experience the joy and rapture of a Romeo and Juliet. Instead, their protestations of love are hedged about with talk of sin, lust and physical violence, and their exchange of vows is couched in ominous terms: 'Love me, or kill me'.

In this scene, Ford develops and extends the play's imagery. Following on from his concluding line in scene 1, Giovanni now acknowledges that he is in the hands of fate rather than God – fate that both 'leads [him] on' and has 'doomed [his] death'. Though he has 'despised' his fate, he recognises that it is his 'destiny' to be loved by Annabella or to die. Thus, the subsequent events of the play acquire a sense of tragic inevitability. 'Blood' continues to feature largely in the dialogue, its associations extended from merely violence and death to include noble birth (Soranzo admits that Grimaldi may be his 'equal in [...] blood'); family relationships (Giovanni talks of his and Annabella's 'Nearness in birth or blood'); and the sense of shame that causes the blood to rush into the cheeks (Giovanni asserts that his sister 'need not blush' to walk with him and notes 'the lily and the rose' alternating on her cheeks, while Annabella admits that she 'blush[es] to tell' Giovanni of her longstanding feelings for him).

Most strikingly, Ford develops the image of the heart – both the symbol of love and the organ that pumps blood around the body. The men of the play are largely concerned with the disposal of Annabella's heart, which Florio tells Soranzo he already possesses (see line 54), not knowing that his daughter regards her heart as 'captive' to her brother. Giovanni's heart is also in question: he will sacrifice it for the sake of admitting his love (lines 157–58), and invites her to 'Rip up [his] bosom' to see his love for her engraved on his heart. This is a shocking premonition of his own physical mutilation of her at the end of the play, in which he demonstrates publicly that Annabella's heart belongs to him.

Act I scene 3

Florio and Donado confirm Bergetto's position as a welcome suitor to Annabella, but Donado despairs of his nephew's stupidity.

This largely comic scene forms an effective interlude between the pre- and post-coital dialogues of Annabella and Giovanni. There is dramatic irony in our knowledge that, while Donado is expending so much energy in pressing his nephew's suit to Annabella, she is engaged elsewhere in sexual intercourse with her brother.

Florio is a more enlightened father than many in Renaissance drama. Unlike Egeus in *A Midsummer Night's Dream* or Capulet in *Romeo and Juliet*, he does not attempt to impose his own choice of husband on his daughter, although it seems he favours Soranzo. If we are to take him at his word, his priority is his daughter's happiness:

> My care is how to match her to her liking:
> I would not have her marry wealth, but love.

The irony is that, unknown to Florio, Annabella's 'liking' is for her own brother, something definitely not catered for in his sense of paternal indulgence.

Bergetto makes a clearer impression in this scene as a likeable idiot, rushing across the stage full of eager anticipation to see the fairground attractions his barber has recommended to him, and not remotely interested in his marriage prospects. He can barely remember the name of the girl in whom he is supposed to be interested, vaguely replying, 'O, the wench' when Donado asks him how his conversation with her went. His report of what he said to her is not promising – Donado finds it 'gross' and 'intolerable' – but she has apparently shown a notable interest in what Bergetto will inherit on his uncle's death, prompting Donado to suggest sending her a letter enclosing 'some rich jewel'. Donado thinks little of his nephew's mental capacity, calling him in the course of the scene 'dunce', 'fool' (twice) and 'ass'. Yet he also refers to him as a 'great baby' and an 'innocent', and it is important that the audience should view Bergetto with the same affectionate, amused indulgence as that apparently shown to him by his servant, Poggio.

Act II scene 1

After their love-making, Giovanni and Annabella reaffirm their feelings for each other. Before he leaves, she promises him she will never marry. She calls Putana, who is by now in their confidence, but the nurse's bawdy commentary is cut short by the arrival of Florio with Richardetto, apparently a doctor from Padua, and his kinswoman Philotis, who are to be on call as physician and companion to Annabella.

Yet again, Ford is indebted to Shakespeare, who brings on both Romeo and Juliet and Troilus and Cressida fresh from their love-making in scenes similar to this. Giovanni is at first serious, then teasing, in his comments on this new stage in their relationship and Annabella's loss of virginity. Briefly, he expresses his love for her in poetically romantic terms (see lines 16–20), before addressing the difficult issue of her apparently imminent marriage prospects. In professing to find all her suitors 'hateful' and promising to live faithful to him alone, Annabella is being somewhat naïve, but understandably so.

At the start of the scene, there is again the potential for shame in their relationship, in Giovanni's exhortation to Annabella, 'Do not blush', and her reply that, if any but her 'heart's delight' had prevailed with her sexually, there might be cause for 'a modest crimson' to be printed on her cheeks. The image of the heart is again emphasised in their dialogue: his heart has been 'inflamed' and offered to her in tribute at the risk of his life; 'keep well my heart', he urges her as he departs. In such a context, even his addressing her with the conventional romantic term 'sweetheart' takes on an extra dimension.

Putana's teasing of Annabella about her loss of virginity is worthy of comment, passing way beyond the bawdy jollity of Juliet's Nurse to reveal an unashamed relish of sexual pleasure, whatever its source – 'father or brother, all is one'. Her agreement with Annabella's wish to keep the relationship secret is not on account of any sense of immorality or shame, but merely to avoid unwelcome gossip. It could be argued that Ford's portrayal of Putana (and indeed Annabella) panders to misogynistic stereotypes of women's unbounded and transgressive sexual appetites, which had to be kept under control, but such misogyny seems to be challenged rather than confirmed by the play as a whole, notably in the questioning irony of the title. It has to be admitted, though, that Putana hardly seems to be a suitable moral guardian for a young woman.

The introduction of Richardetto and Philotis is an intriguing development; the fact that Ford takes some care in explaining their role indicates that they are to play a key part in the plot, though it is impossible for the audience to predict what that might be. Easily missed, though, is Florio's comment that Annabella has 'of late been sickly', explaining the need to have a physician readily available. Clearly, her health is to become a significant element of the play.

Act II scene 2

Soranzo is interrupted in his composition of love poetry to Annabella by the intrusion of Hippolita, the widow, with whom he had an affair while her husband was still alive. She launches into a passionate attack on him for failing to honour his promise to marry her in the event of her husband's death, the circumstances of which she recounts. Vasques attempts to mediate between them, but Soranzo leaves after condemning Hippolita's lust and wickedness. Vasques promises to aid Hippolita in her revenge, but he is not taken in by her vow to reward him with her love.

With the main plot well underway, Ford turns his attention to the subplot, linked to it through Soranzo's romantic aspirations towards Annabella that, judging by the opening of the scene, seem genuine. He is reading a poem expressing the pains of love, rephrasing it to convey instead love's joys, which he claims to have experienced at first hand through his feelings for Annabella. Hippolita's intrusion disrupts his romantic reflections, and her outburst plunges the play into melodrama, emphasised by certain persistent rhetorical features of her speech. First, there is her use of imperatives, or commands: 'Look, perjured man'; 'Know, Soranzo'; 'Call me not dear'; 'tell her thus'. Then there is her employment of rhetorical questions, as at lines 26, 29–30, and 38–41, the third of these forcefully answered by herself: 'No!' She addresses Soranzo twice as 'perjured man' and also as 'false wanton', terms which combine with her passionate and inflated imagery – 'distracted lust', 'sensual rage of blood', 'the charms / Of hell or sorcery' – to create the air of exaggerated emotional outrage that lends her speech its melodramatic quality.

We have heard previously, from Putana, of Hippolita's former relationship with Soranzo (see I.2.92–94), but in case we have forgotten, Ford now gives us a more detailed account from Hippolita herself. She claims that Soranzo seduced her, 'Against the honour of [her] chaster bosom' and vowed to marry her in the event of her husband's death. Hence, she now feels betrayed by Soranzo's abandonment of her, to fulfil his lustful desires on a woman of inferior social class, scornfully referring to Annabella as 'Your goodly Madam Merchant'. What is less clear is her account of her husband's death, and in what sense Soranzo himself was partly responsible for it. She first suggests that her husband's death was 'urged on by his disgrace', in other words, partly induced by the shock of her unfaithfulness to him, and therefore that it is Soranzo who has effectively 'divorced / My husband from his life'. Later, she confesses that she herself urged her husband 'to undertake / A voyage to Leghorn' with a view to precipitating his death, and that he did indeed die 'on the way', so that he '[bought] his death so dear / With [her] advice'. None of this makes much sense unless we know that the journey of 80 miles from Parma to Leghorn was potentially dangerous, though Hippolita's sense of guilt still seems rather unnecessary. Soranzo plays on it, though, not only in confirming her guilt in 'bringing of a gentleman to death / Who was thy husband', but in praising, perhaps sarcastically, that husband's qualities in 'Learning, behaviour, entertainment, love, / As Parma could not show a braver man'. All this would be clearer if the cause of the husband's death were actually specified. We might, however, note that the journey to Leghorn was to bring back his recently orphaned niece, and that in the previous scene a doctor and his young 'cousin', apparently from Padua, were introduced into Florio's household.

Soranzo is now the object of revenge by two characters, Grimaldi (see I.2.47) and Hippolita, whose 'vengeance' gains apparent support from Vasques at the end of this scene. At first, Vasques seems to offer Hippolita good advice in urging her to renew her suit to Soranzo on the next day 'in some milder temper', but she convinces him that the reward for his service will be 'Beggary and neglect' and persuades him to assist her in 'bring[ing] to pass a plot' to further her revenge; in return, she will give him herself and all she has. We are likely to be struck by her naïvety in trusting Vasques, whom we have already seen prepared to risk his life in defending his master's honour against Grimaldi's slanders. If we were in any doubt of his true intentions, Ford reveals in Vasques's aside at line 141 that he knows exactly what Hippolita is up to. Vasques's own performance skills are emphasised by his fondness for theatrical metaphor, when he disparages the way Soranzo has dealt with Hippolita, commenting 'This part has been scurvily played', and when he agrees to be 'a special actor' in Hippolita's revenge plot. We are left with the expectation that he will double-cross her in the service of his master.

Act II scene 3

It is revealed that the 'Doctor' is, in fact, Hippolita's husband, who is believed dead. He explains to his niece, Philotis, that he has adopted the disguise in order to observe his wife's behaviour. He also questions Philotis, now Annabella's companion, about Annabella's feelings towards Soranzo, who seems almost certain to be married to her. They are interrupted by Grimaldi, who asks the 'Doctor' for love potions to win Annabella's affection. Instead, Richardetto informs him that he must first remove his rival, Soranzo, in which he promises to assist him.

A third revenge motive now enters the play, as Richardetto contrives the killing of Soranzo, the man who has dishonoured him through his adultery with Hippolita. Though Philotis suspects something of his intentions, he keeps her in ignorance for her own safety. In performance, the revelation of Richardetto's true identity needs careful handling so that the audience is left in no doubt of who he is. The simplest way is for him to remove his doctor's disguise – possibly a false beard and glasses – at the start of the scene, and hastily resume it on his line 'I am the Doctor now', as he becomes aware of Grimaldi's approach.

In pursuing revenge on his wife and her former lover, Richardetto is alert to all information that may help to further his interests. Perhaps this is why he seems so interested in Philotis's report that Annabella seems as indifferent to Soranzo, her prospective husband, as to any other man. 'There's mystery in that which time must show', Richardetto comments, helping to build up a sense of suspense in relation to the possible discovery of Annabella's incest.

Once again, the question of who Annabella's heart belongs to is central to the play. 'Soranzo is the man that hath her heart', Richardetto tells Grimaldi, confirming Florio's earlier words to Soranzo (see I.2.54); however, he knows from Philotis that this is not true – at least if we assume that having Annabella's heart signifies being the object of her love. The play shows, however, that having her heart is much more about masculine possessiveness: to have Annabella's heart would put Soranzo in control of her – and, of course, the dowry she brings with her on her marriage.

Grimaldi's visit to the Doctor in search of a love potion to secure Annabella's affections seems strange to us, but plays of the period, even serious ones, are full of such fairytale plot devices, such as the sleeping-draught with which Friar Lawrence simulates Juliet's death. More interesting is the ruthlessness with which Richardetto and Grimaldi plan Soranzo's murder by poisoned rapier. Grimaldi, it appears, is a man with powerful connections, now attending on the Cardinal, the Pope's representative in Parma. Richardetto's suggestion that his assisting of Grimaldi in Soranzo's death might be regarded as a favour to the Cardinal (see line 55) hardly places the Church in a positive moral light, preparing us for the Cardinal's dubious role in subsequent events. It is noteworthy, too, that Grimaldi never questions Richardetto's motives in helping him, merely asking 'But shall I trust thee, Doctor?' In common with other characters in the play, Richardetto entrusts the outcome of events to 'the fates' – an odd invocation in a play set in a supposedly Catholic society, perhaps indicating a tension between lingering pagan beliefs and Christian faith. This is illustrated too in the way Giovanni is torn between his fate and the religious authority of the Friar.

Act II scene 4

Donado has written a letter to Annabella on his nephew's behalf, but Bergetto has composed one on his own account. As Donado leaves to deliver the letter, Bergetto and Poggio ignore his instructions to stay indoors, and set off to see the fairground attractions.

Bergetto's genial stupidity leaves his uncle amusingly at his wit's end, and provides an entertaining foil to the play's more serious concerns. It is important that we should like Bergetto and find him harmless; his insistence on his own intelligence and maturity ('O, you think I am a blockhead, uncle!'; 'Dost take me for a child, Poggio?') can be quite touching, as can his relationship with Poggio. If Bergetto's bawdy remarks seem to make his character more coarse, at least those in the letter ('I can board where I see occasion'; 'commending my best parts to you'; 'Yours upwards and downwards') can be ascribed to Poggio's assistance in composing it, with Bergetto entirely innocent of their double meanings. A young man who is more excited at the prospect of seeing the 'horse with the head in's tail' than in wooing an attractive young woman is a child indeed.

Act II scene 5

Giovanni has confessed to the Friar that he has had sex with Annabella. The Friar is horrified, predicts a disastrous outcome, and condemns Giovanni's attempts to justify his actions by reasoned argument. The Friar suggests that Annabella should be persuaded to marry or, since Giovanni objects to this, at least to come to him to confess and be absolved. Giovanni agrees, but even the threat of eternal torment fails to shake his passion for his sister.

There is absolutely no meeting of minds between Giovanni and the Friar in this scene: they seem to inhabit entirely different moral universes. The Friar's world is one of divine retribution, in which 'Heaven is angry' and Giovanni is, as a consequence, 'sold to hell'. The only hope is in prayer, and in trusting to 'The throne of mercy', which could yet operate if only Giovanni would renounce his sin. Giovanni is blind to all this, however, and puts the Friar's failure to understand his love for Annabella down to his age, which is incapable of appreciating his sister's beauty. Giovanni blasphemously sets up this beauty as a rival deity to the Christian God:

> Your age o'errules you; had you youth like mine,
> You'd make her love your heaven, and her divine.

Giovanni continues to rely on the philosophical debating skills for which the Friar berated him in the play's opening lines, 'proving' to his own satisfaction that, since physical beauty is invariably matched by virtue of mind, Annabella must be virtuous; and since love is the 'quintessence' of virtue, her love for him, and by reflection his for her, must be virtuous. His arguments are superficial and specious, however, as the Friar bitterly points out: 'O ignorance in knowledge!'

As well as his debating skill, Giovanni also demonstrates his poetic sensibilities. His speech in praise of Annabella (lines 49–58) is modelled on a familiar technique of love poetry, the blazon, in which the poet catalogues his mistress's qualities from head to toe in a series of comparisons. Blazons were often constructed in sonnet form, a typical example being Edmund Spenser's 'Ye tradeful Merchants', in which he castigates those who seek abroad for precious things, since they are all contained within his mistress. Shakespeare mocks the elaborate artificiality of the blazon in his Sonnet 130, 'My mistress' eyes are nothing like the sun'. The coyly suggestive conclusion of Giovanni's effort is emphasised by the use of a rhyming couplet. In fact, the Friar and Giovanni employ rhyming couplets twice each during the scene, perhaps suggesting a certain superficiality in their arguments, particularly when Giovanni caps the Friar's couplet in lines 33–36.

Act II scene 6

Annabella tells her father that Giovanni has gone to see the Friar. Donado delivers Bergetto's letter to Annabella; Putana claims to Donado that she is encouraging her mistress to look kindly on Bergetto. Annabella tries to avoid reading the letter, but her father insists. Her response to it is equivocal, and she offers to return the jewel enclosed with it. Florio suggests she should send to Bergetto the ring bequeathed to her by her mother, destined to be given only to her first husband, but she says Giovanni took it from her to wear that day. Forced to respond to Bergetto's letter, she rejects his suit; Donado accepts her refusal with a good grace just as his nephew appears with Poggio. Bergetto reports that he has just been injured in a street encounter and had his wounds dressed by a newly arrived doctor and his niece, whom he much prefers to Annabella. Donado departs with Bergetto and Poggio, leaving the jewel as a gift for Annabella when she marries. Giovanni returns, and Florio reports Annabella's rejection of Bergetto, commending Soranzo as his own choice for her. Giovanni responds with jealousy as he questions his sister about the jewel Donado has left with her.

This scene, though apparently straightforward, raises a number of questions of character-isation, staging and interpretation. First, there is the question of which letter Donado delivers to Annabella — the one written by Bergetto himself, or that written by Donado on his behalf. Perhaps, in staging, we could see Donado choosing between the two letters at the end of II.4, deciding on one of them and enclosing the jewel he mentioned at I.3.81. His own letter is the more likely choice; in any event, Annabella gives no indication in her response that she has just read Bergetto's ludicrous composition.

Second, there is the matter of Annabella's ring, which she says Giovanni took from her that morning. Although there is nothing in the text of II.1 to indicate this, perhaps the giving of the ring could be incorporated into the staging of that scene, with Giovanni then wearing it in his scene with the Friar, II.5. More important, though, is the sexual significance of the ring: colloquially, a woman's 'ring' referred to her vagina. Emblematically, then, the ring that Annabella is 'not to give [...] / To any but [her] husband' represents her virginity, and in saying that her brother took it from her she effectively confesses her incest. This would be understood by Ford's audience, but the characters in the scene would, of course, respond only to the literal meaning of her words.

Florio's character is also worthy of note, and the actor needs to decide on the extent of his hypocrisy in seeming to promote Bergetto's claims as suitor to his daughter, when we know his preferred choice is Soranzo — something he confirms later in the scene. Perhaps he is merely buttering up Donado, not wishing to risk losing his friendship. Putana's motives are at least more open, as she blatantly lies to Donado for financial reward.

As for Bergetto himself, he has now discovered attractions elsewhere, in the form of the Doctor's niece. His account of the circumstances of his meeting with her, and the way he tells Annabella to her face that her own beauty is far inferior, again reveal an innocent comic stupidity, as does his response on learning that Annabella has turned him down. However, the contrast between Bergetto and Giovanni, who enters as he leaves, is not entirely to the latter's advantage. His irritable jealousy on seeing the jewel Donado has left with his sister makes him seem petulant and possessive, while Annabella's amused response, both to Bergetto and to her brother, makes her a far more sympathetic character.

Act III scene 1

Bergetto insists to Poggio that he is determined to marry the Doctor's niece, in spite of his uncle's objections.

Bergetto is more assertive in this scene; clearly Philotis has made a deep impression on him and apparently he is assured both of her love — she has given him presents — and of her uncle's approval. We are left to wonder what Donado objects to in the relationship, since he expressed no particular reservations in the previous scene. Presumably, it is a question of Philotis's social inferiority; at any rate, it is important for the plot that Bergetto plans to arrange a secret marriage with her.

Act III scene 2

Florio openly expresses his approval of Soranzo as a prospective husband for Annabella, and leaves them alone together, but Giovanni observes in secret from the upper level. Annabella rejects Soranzo's courtship, and her mocking tone annoys him. She tells him of her determination to remain unmarried, but says he is the only man she would consider if the necessity arose. Suddenly she feels unwell and faints, and is hurried off to bed by Florio, Putana and Giovanni while the Doctor is sent for. Soranzo confides in Vasques what Annabella has said to him.

The pressures on Annabella become acute in this scene, even though Florio is not forcing her to accept Soranzo as a husband. For the audience, Giovanni's spying on Soranzo and Annabella's conversation enhances the sense of the constraints under which his sister is operating; he has already told her, in a hastily snatched aside, not to be 'all woman' but to think of him – a remark that, in its misogyny and selfishness, enhances the negative impression he creates. His comments to himself – or to the audience – as he eavesdrops suggest an almost gloating relish of how her love for him is confirmed by her sharp responses to Soranzo, but as she falls suddenly ill he is thrown into a panic, rushing down to tend to her.

Annabella's role in the scene is an interesting one for an actor to play. Her situation is a delicate and dangerous one, since she must refuse Soranzo without admitting to any other relationship. She is given no words in response to Giovanni's injunction to her at line 11, and an actor must decide whether she would risk a non-verbal response of some kind – a look, a smile, a press of the hand. Initially, her strategy with Soranzo is to exchange light, witty banter, though she is forced into one direct lie, in vowing 'To live and die a maid', in other words a virgin. When Soranzo becomes more pressing, demanding that she 'leave those fruitless strifes of wit', she at first becomes even more jokey, calling for medicine to relieve his professed lovesickness, but his failure to get the message forces her to be more straightforward in explaining that she does not love him. Mistakenly, perhaps, she goes a stage further, attempting to soften the blow by admitting that he is the only one of her suitors she would have considered accepting. She ends by appealing to his virtue, nobility and love in asking him not to reveal to her father what she has said to him.

It is an effective dramatic surprise when Annabella is suddenly taken ill, though we have heard previously of her delicate health (II.1.54–55). Perhaps, at this stage, we might put her fainting fit down to the emotional pressure of her situation, but Vasques has an alternative diagnosis. Partly to encourage his master, he suggests that Annabella is suffering from an excess of adolescent sexual need, a condition easily remedied by marriage and its physical consummation. The problem here is that Soranzo is not entirely clear whether Annabella has rejected him outright. Ford also gives Vasques a line, spoken aside to the audience, that reminds them of the simmering subplot of Hippolita's revenge. He observes that Soranzo's 'life's in danger' as well as Annabella's, and we recall that he has ostensibly agreed to assist Hippolita in her scheme.

Soranzo himself creates a mixed impression in this scene. Although Annabella appeals to his 'virtue' and 'noble courses', these are not qualities suggested by his appearances so far in the play. As for his love for Annabella, although he claims to have 'loved [her] long, and loved [her] truly', we might consider his claim, 'Not hope of what you have, but what you are / Have drawn me on' as being distinctly disingenuous. What Annabella has, from Soranzo's point of view, is a rich father, a fact which presumably outweighs her own attractions and overrides her family's social inferiority. Soranzo is plainly at a loss in interpreting Annabella's response to him; at first he humours her wit, then her 'scornful taunts' make him cross, and he is left unclear as to whether she has given him 'an absolute denial'. Though we may find his confusion amusing, he is not a sympathetic character, and his references to his 'heart' at lines 24 and 36 carry a physicality that works against their supposedly romantic implications. In terms of the play's imagery, the first of these references, with Annabella's witty response, prefigures the play's gory conclusion.

Act III scene 3

Putana tells Giovanni that Annabella is pregnant. He tells her to keep the Doctor away from his sister, and to tell their father that she has recovered.

Putana's worldly experience is evident in her instant diagnosis of what is wrong with Annabella, and in the explicit language in which she describes her symptoms – though she is mysteriously coy in referring to 'another thing that I could name'. Her selfishness is also apparent: she expresses no feelings of sympathy for her mistress, blames Giovanni for the situation even though she herself gleefully encouraged their incest, and worries principally about the consequences for herself: 'Heaven help us!'

The natural assumption would be that Giovanni is horrified by the news of his sister's pregnancy, but in the 1991 RSC production, Jonathan Cullen as Giovanni was overcome with joy, as well as by the perplexity the text demands. With the delighted excitement of the prospective father, Giovanni jumped backwards, according to the reviewer Harry Eyres, 'like toast ejecting from an overenthusiastic toaster'. His state of mind, as he rapidly runs through how to deal with the situation, is well-captured by the quick-fire verse in which he gives Putana her instructions, contrasting with the prose of the rest of the scene.

Act III scene 4

Richardetto, the false Doctor, has examined Annabella and reports to Florio that she has now recovered. He diagnoses her symptoms as being provoked by sexual frustration, for which marriage would be the best cure. Florio determines to have the Friar marry her urgently to Soranzo. The Friar himself arrives with Giovanni, who has brought him to visit the sick Annabella. Florio asks the Friar to urge Annabella to marry.

It is not clear how the Doctor has been allowed to see Annabella, contrary to Giovanni's instructions in the previous scene. His diagnosis of her state, though, matches that of Vasques, who had earlier suggested she was suffering from 'the maid's sickness, an overflux of youth' (III.2.80–81) – what Richardetto now calls 'a fullness of her blood'. As the New Mermaids editor suggests in the footnotes, some young virgins were thought to suffer from a kind of overdeveloped sexuality that could make them ill if left unfulfilled. Florio obviously understands immediately what the Doctor is referring to, and his remedy is the same as that earlier suggested by Vasques – to get Annabella married, and her sexual needs satisfied, as soon as possible. All this seems very strange to the modern reader.

The Doctor is, of course, mistaken in his diagnosis – but then, he is not a real doctor, raising questions about his role that Ford does not answer. Is he simply wrong about Annabella's condition, failing to realise that she is pregnant? Or does he, having correctly identified her condition, conceal it in order to encourage her marriage to Soranzo? Marriage to a woman who later proved to be pregnant by another man would be a shameful experience, and would enhance Richardetto's revenge on Soranzo. However, since

Richardetto is already plotting Soranzo's death, perhaps tricking him into a humiliating marriage would be irrelevant to his purposes. Whatever the actor decides, the audience is likely to be none the wiser, so perhaps the issue is academic.

Giovanni has presumably told the Friar of Annabella's pregnancy, and brought him to her to offer comfort and advice. Florio's greeting of the Friar is a conventional one, but his praise of him as 'one /That still bring blessing to the place you come to' is worth matching against our own judgement of the Friar as the play develops. He is in a particularly acute moral dilemma at this point, balancing the confidentiality of the confessional (which means he is bound to conceal from Florio the knowledge of his children's incest) with his Christian responsibility to condemn their sin; and attempting to reconcile the fact of Annabella's pregnancy by her brother with Florio's urging of him to counsel marriage. The actor has a great deal of anxiety to convey in the Friar's short appearance in this scene.

Act III scene 5

Grimaldi waits for the Doctor to bring the poison for the plot against Soranzo's life, which he soon does; but he also brings news that Soranzo is to be betrothed, and possibly married, to Annabella that night, and recommends that Grimaldi lies in wait to assault his victim in the vicinity of the Friar's cell. Gloating on his imminent revenge, Richardetto calls Philotis, who says she has taken his advice to love Bergetto and will marry him that night, to avoid his uncle, Donado, finding out and preventing them. Bergetto arrives with Poggio, the lovers exchange kisses, and Richardetto urges haste in enacting their marriage.

This scene, like the previous one, is principally important in moving the narrative forward. It is a scene of secrets and conspiracies: the plot to kill Soranzo; the hasty betrothal between Soranzo and Annabella; the secret engagement of Philotis and Bergetto. This needs to be reflected in the playing and pacing of the scene, but it is important that each key plot development should be clearly communicated to the audience. There is an element of melodrama in the characterisation of both Grimaldi and Richardetto, reflected in the gloating tone of their language: 'if this physician / Play not on both hands, then Soranzo falls'; 'So, if this hit, I'll laugh and hug revenge'. The melodramatic plotting of these two is contrasted with the rather touching relationship between Philotis and Bergetto, and the latter's comic sexual naïvety in not identifying the 'swelling about [his] stomach' as an erection provoked by kissing her. It is important for future developments that Philotis shows genuine affection for Bergetto. Even though she has followed her uncle's advice in 'Fashion[ing] [her] heart to love him', her comment 'There's hope of this yet' should be played to indicate her enjoyment of their kiss, and her acceptance of their relationship on her own account; (not grasping the point of this line, some editors of the play have given it instead to either Richardetto or Poggio). By the end of the scene we are led to expect two imminent marriages at the Friar's cell, and an attack on Soranzo with a poisoned rapier.

Act III scene 6

Annabella expresses her repentance to the Friar, who preaches to her of the torments of hell, which she can avoid if she marries Soranzo and is faithful to him, abandoning her love for her brother. She agrees, Soranzo is brought in and their betrothal is celebrated by the Friar. Giovanni reflects on the Friar's betrayal of him.

Though the opening stage direction indicates that the scene is set in the Friar's cell, it seems more logical for it to take place in Annabella's chamber, where the Friar was escorted to talk to her at the end of III.4. This would mean that Grimaldi's plan to assault Soranzo at the Friar's cell would be thwarted, and perhaps explains the case of mistaken identity that occurs in the next scene. Perhaps, as Simon Barker suggests, the Friar 'in his study' means simply that he is engaged in deep contemplation as the scene opens.

The Friar's lecture to Annabella is a terrifying catalogue of eternal damnation with which churchgoers would be familiar. He summarises the torment meted out to gluttons, drunkards, usurers and murderers, building up to the 'racks of burning steel' that await those guilty of lust, and the eternity of mutual reproach to be endured by the 'wretched things / Who have dreamt out whole years in lawless sheets / And secret incests'. Such sermons worked through instilling fear rather than by promoting moral virtue for its own sake, and it is hardly surprising that the Friar notes signs of repentance in Annabella. The Friar's remedy, however, is questionable. He seems primarily concerned with her 'honour's safety' and only secondarily with saving her soul, but his urging her to marry Soranzo seems neither sensible nor morally justifiable. Partly, he is bowing to pressure from Florio in encouraging the marriage, and he seems unaware of the risks of Soranzo finding out that he is not the father of his wife's child. He is naïve, too, in believing that Annabella can renounce Giovanni; even though he acknowledges that 'the baits of sin / Are hard to leave', he does not consider the strength of the love between brother and sister. Looking back from the perspective of the play's ending, we can again find its gory climax prefigured in the violent physicality of the Friar's outraged exclamation that Annabella has 'unripped a soul so foul and guilty', and his more conciliatory observation of 'New motions in [her] heart'.

The rest of the scene seems positively rushed: in the space of merely ten lines that are shared mostly between two speakers, which increases the pace, the Friar confirms that Soranzo has agreed to the marriage and performs the formal betrothal between him and Annabella, while Giovanni bitterly reflects on 'this Friar's falsehood'. It is up to the actors to register, through facial expression, movement, positioning and body language, the characters' unspoken feelings during this brief sequence. Florio, presumably, is delighted, while Giovanni fumes; Soranzo cannot believe his luck, but Vasques perhaps registers suspicion at this hasty turnaround; the Friar probably exhibits enormous relief, but with an undercurrent of apprehension; while Annabella, 'weeping', has the difficult task of suppressing her desperate unhappiness and presenting an image of modest compliance.

Act III scene 7

Lying in wait for Soranzo, Grimaldi mistakenly stabs Bergetto with the poisoned rapier when he and Philotis pass by on the way to their secret wedding. Richardetto sends Poggio off for help and he returns with officers, who then go in search of the attacker. Bergetto dies and his body is removed by his mourning companions.

This is a brilliant and shocking scene – shocking partly because the killing of Bergetto is at first treated comically. It is a perfect example of how dramatists of Ford's period mix violence and laughter to create an ambivalent response in the audience.

If we assume that the betrothal of Soranzo and Annabella took place at Florio's house, not at the Friar's cell as originally planned, then Grimaldi's mistake in identifying the disguised couple seems inevitable. Richardetto's culpability in Bergetto's death should not be forgotten, since he encouraged Grimaldi's revenge on Soranzo, provided the poison for the rapier, and told the murderer where to lie in wait. It is not clear from the scene whether he realises what has gone wrong, and that it is Grimaldi who has stabbed Bergetto, and it is up to the actor to register Richardetto's gradual apprehension of the truth.

The fact that Bergetto's response to his stabbing is couched in the language of his usual comic naïvety, so that he doesn't quite realise what has happened to him, is perhaps intended to mislead the audience into thinking that this likeable, childish idiot is hardly going to be killed off. Audiences invariably laugh at his response to his injuries beyond the point where it ceases to be comic, so that they are then brought up short by the guilty realisation that, actually, it is not funny at all. His final speech, coupled with the reactions of the other characters, transforms him from a comic into a tragic character, and the simplicity of Poggio's heartfelt lament, 'O my master, my master, my master!' is intensely moving in performance. Ford's manipulation of our responses is both cunning and skilful.

Act III scene 8

Vasques informs Hippolita of Soranzo and Annabella's betrothal, and she plans her revenge to coincide with their wedding in two days' time. She promises herself to Vasques as his reward for serving as her accomplice.

This brief scene serves to remind us that, though one revenge plot against Soranzo has miscarried, there is another in the offing. Though there is nothing in the dialogue to suggest that Vasques is planning to double-cross Hippolita, there is scope for the actor to indicate this, perhaps through an exaggerated sincerity in his delivery of the lines, or glances shared with the audience, or his facial expression as they – presumably – embrace at line 17. The differences in their social status are drawn to our attention when Vasques emphasises his loyalty, saying he is hardly likely to betray her when she offers him 'so hopeful a preferment' – in other words, social advancement through marrying her. She could also be referring to this when she promises 'I will be thine in spite of my disgrace' – the disgrace, presumably, of marrying a social inferior. Such concerns with class and social mobility are subtly delineated throughout the play.

Act III scene 9

Florio urges Donado to seek justice for his nephew's murder. An officer reports that the murderer, identified as Grimaldi, has taken sanctuary with the Cardinal. They knock on the Cardinal's gate, and he and Grimaldi emerge. Grimaldi confesses that he killed Bergetto in mistake for Soranzo, and the Cardinal receives him into the Pope's protection, refusing all pleas for justice. Donado and Florio are outraged.

The key word of this scene is justice, both an abstract concept and, with a capital J, a deity who, as in classical mythology, has abandoned the earth and 'fled to heaven'. The ties of 'blood' or noble birth take precedence over moral and religious law in the actions of the Cardinal, who begins by demonstrating contempt for Florio and Donado on account of their inferior social status, calling them 'saucy mates' and suggesting they are treating his residence as a 'common inn'. He goes on to stress Grimaldi's aristocratic origins as one 'nobly born / Of princes' blood', whom Florio thought 'too mean a husband' for Annabella. The Cardinal's arrogance is matched by an utter lack of sympathy for Donado's grief: 'Is that your business?' he demands, referring contemptuously to Bergetto's death, and brusquely concludes, 'Bury your dead'. He speaks of himself mostly in the royal plural, and his verse has a sonorous regularity that matches his supreme self-confidence as 'Nuncio from the Pope'.

In his portrayal of the Cardinal, Ford is offering a stinging attack on the Catholic Church, a familiar object of satirical mockery in the drama of his time. It is crucial that we remember the Cardinal's role in this scene when we come to his dispensing of judgement at the end of the play. The responses of Donado and Florio make explicit the play's moral attitude to the Cardinal: 'Is this a churchman's voice?' Donado demands, while Florio bewails a world in which 'cardinals think murder's not amiss'. Florio's concluding couplet, one of the most striking in the play, sums up both the corruption of power and the ultimate justice of heaven.

Grimaldi's speech offers the actor a choice of whether to suggest genuine sorrow and repentance for Bergetto's death, or merely a show of hypocritical piety. It is interesting that he confesses his revenge plot against Soranzo, and that the Cardinal offers not the slightest hint of moral judgement on Grimaldi's actions – a striking contrast with his attitude at the end of the play.

Poggio's role in the scene is disappointingly slight in view of his moving outburst of grief at the end of III.7. Perhaps his offer to knock at the gate gives him a chance to relieve his sorrow and anger; judging by the Cardinal's comment at lines 32–33 his knocking is certainly forceful. At least two modern directors have enhanced Poggio's role here by emphasising his grief, frustration and anger. In the 1977 RSC production, he was left alone on stage at the end of the scene, shaking the iron gates of the Cardinal's house in his rage. In 1991, also at the RSC, Poggio responded to the Church's denial of justice for his master's murder by tearing off his crucifix, throwing it to the ground and spitting on it. In both productions, the interval was taken at the end of this scene – an effective placing, but not the only option.

Act IV scene 1

The guests gather for Soranzo and Annabella's wedding banquet. Vasques notes that Giovanni seems unwell, and Florio urges Donado to put his nephew's death behind him. Giovanni refuses to drink a toast to the marriage. A group of ladies perform a masque in honour of the wedding; Hippolita reveals herself as one of them, pretends to give her blessing to the marriage and drinks to Soranzo. As he is about to drink too, Vasques interrupts, informs Hippolita that he has given her the poisoned cup, and reveals to the company the revenge she was planning on Soranzo. Hippolita dies cursing Soranzo and Annabella as the banquet breaks up in confusion.

In its combination of spectacle and horror, this extravagant scene is typical of the revenge drama of Ford's period. In particular, the performance of a play or a masque as a front for the enactment of revenge had become something of a cliché and, as here, often ran the risk of arousing audience laughter. This is the second time in the play when a formal banquet is disrupted by violence, the first being when Florio's dinner for Annabella's suitors was disturbed by Grimaldi's fight with Vasques. A third such occasion will mark the play's tragic climax.

The imagery of the scene moves from heaven to hell, from the Friar's celebration of the 'holy rites' and the invisible presence of 'the saints' at the feast, to Hippolita's suffering from 'Heat above hell-fire!' and 'cruel, cruel flames!' The Friar's religious complacency is a sham, however, as we know only too well, and hell is present in the imagery from the start, in Giovanni's anguished contemplation of 'the horror of ten thousand deaths'. Soranzo's complacency is more mercenary; he sees his new wife as a possession – a 'precious jewel' and 'a prize'. At the start of the scene he is the joyful bridegroom, completely unaware of the irony as he joshingly warns Giovanni 'Your turn comes next'. Whatever he feels in response to his brother-in-law's refusal to drink is cut short by the arrival of the masquers.

Hippolita's role in this scene is a showy one for an actor, moving as it does from the choreographed physicality of the dance, through the gloating, false sincerity of her apparent blessing of Soranzo and Annabella's marriage, to the anguish of her death throes and the extravagant melodrama of her curses. There are many sources of potential laughter in this sequence, and a director will need to decide how appropriate such a response is. The essential source of humour lies in the sudden recoiling of Hippolita's revenge upon herself, thanks to Vasques's cool double-crossing. To modern sensibilities, the chorus-like exclamations of the assembled company: 'Hippolita!'; 'What's the matter?'; 'Wonderful justice!', are potentially ludicrous, while the disguised Richardetto's simplistic moral judgements, 'Heaven, thou art righteous' and 'Here's the end / Of lust and pride' seem pompous and hypocritical in view of his own involvement in a revenge plot that has tragically miscarried.

Annabella has only two lines in the scene, but her very silence can be used powerfully by a skilful actor to suggest her emotional state. At the start of the scene, she has been trapped by circumstances, including the social and religious pressures put on her by her father and the Friar, into marrying a man for whom she has no feelings, and whose reaction when he discovers she is pregnant can only be imagined. In addition, she has to suppress her love for her brother and contemplate his bitterness at the wedding feast, terrified in case his behaviour should betray their relationship. Her urging of Soranzo not to insist that Giovanni should toast the couple's happiness is tactful and low-key, but must conceal the anguish she is going through. By the end of the scene, the horror Annabella feels at her situation has been externalised in the appalling events of Hippolita's gruesome death, and she and her marriage have been viciously and publicly cursed. Her only comment, 'It is a fearful sight', can barely represent what she is feeling. In the 1991 RSC production, Saskia Reeves's Annabella was by this point in a state of complete physical and emotional collapse.

The rhyming couplet with which the Friar ends the scene is worth a close look, since it often gets a laugh in performance. At first glance, it may appear to be its melodramatic quality, emphasised by the four alliterative bs, that makes it seem rather comic. However, there is something inherently ludicrous in the statement itself: one wonders how many times the Friar has experienced similar bloody events at a 'bride-banquet', in order to be able to make such a generalisation. The qualifying adverb, 'seldom', simply exacerbates the comic effect: one can hardly imagine how a marriage could *ever* recover from such a bloody beginning. The effect is one of bathos, and it is impossible to judge just how deliberate it is.

Act IV scene 2

Richardetto reflects on his wife's shame and her death and renounces his revenge on Soranzo, convinced that God will punish his enemy for his sins. He reports to Philotis rumours of dissension within Soranzo and Annabella's marriage, and advises his niece to renounce the world and enter a nunnery in Cremona.

This scene conveys a sense of the passage of time – long enough for rumours to have spread abroad about Annabella and Soranzo's marriage difficulties. It also marks the conclusion of the subplot concerning Richardetto and Philotis – though, as he promises, he remains in Parma to observe the outcome of events, or what he calls 'the end of these extremes'. It is rare in the drama of the period for a revenger to abandon his revenge, but that is what Richardetto does here. Partly, he predicts that Soranzo's eventual punishment will be largely self-inflicted, so that he will 'sink with his own weight', and partly he recognises that justice resides in heaven, where 'there is one / Above begins to work'. How convinced we are by Richardetto's conversion to an alternative moral ethos is debatable, but in reflecting on his own actions as well as recommending to his niece the life of a nun, he certainly seems to have become convinced that 'No life is blessèd but the way to heaven'.

Philotis ends her role in the play as she began it, subject to her uncle's will. Her line 'Uncle, shall I resolve to be a nun?' can be delivered to express either resigned acceptance or horrified surprise, but ultimately she has little choice but to follow her uncle's advice. Since in other plays of the period, such as *A Midsummer Night's Dream* and *Hamlet*, the prospect of entering a nunnery is not held out as an attractive option, it is difficult to view

Philotis as anything other than the victim of a patriarchal society, in which women's choices are limited and determined by men.

Act IV scene 3

Having discovered that Annabella is pregnant, Soranzo drags her in, abuses and threatens her, and demands to know the identity of the father, which she withholds. Vasques defends Annabella from Soranzo's wrath and gets him to calm down, secretly promising to find out the identity of Annabella's lover. Soranzo feigns forgiveness towards Annabella and sends her to her room. Vasques confirms that he will discover the information needed for Soranzo to be revenged, and tricks Putana into revealing the truth. In return, he has her taken away by a gang of thugs, ordering them to put out her eyes. Giovanni appears, and Vasques tells him his sister is ill and directs him to her room. Soranzo returns, having treated Annabella gently but still burning for revenge. Vasques takes him off to tell him in private what he has learned.

Two revenge plots have miscarried and one has been abandoned, but in this scene another is set in motion. 'Revenge' and 'vengeance' are key words in the scene, in a surprising variety of contexts. Annabella claims that if Soranzo kills her she will 'leave revenge behind' to pursue him, presumably in the person of her brother. Soranzo, though, retorts that he 'will not slack [his] vengeance' and later declares that his 'blood / Is fired in swift revenge'. Vasques persuades him to 'smother [his] revenge', and Soranzo reluctantly admits that 'Delay in vengeance gives a heavier blow' – and, presumably, a greater sense of satisfaction to the revenger. Vasques clearly regards himself as a connoisseur, who must 'tutor [Soranzo] better in his points of vengeance', but his master's impatience continues to fire his frustration, in which his 'soul / Runs circular in sorrow for revenge!' Such a range of references marks revenge as a key theme of the play, and we are led to question its motivation, its morality, its practical application, its effect on both revenger and victim, and whether it ultimately achieves anything.

Equally insistent in the scene is the range of abusive epithets that Soranzo applies to Annabella, all suggestive of her sexual incontinency. In the misogynistic culture of the time, women's supposedly voracious sexual appetites were a common cause of male anxiety, and Soranzo would be particularly outraged to discover that such a young, apparently virginal wife is not only sexually experienced but is about to make him the father of another man's child. The standard term of sexual abuse is the one used in the play's title, 'whore', to which Soranzo resorts a number of times, along with a range of synonyms such as 'strumpet', 'harlot' and 'quean' as well as more generally abusive designations such as 'Damnable monster'. For him, Annabella is the ultimate in sexual depravity, the 'Whore of whores', guilty of 'lust' and 'luxury' (lechery). Having been calmed down by Vasques, he nevertheless delights in telling her that she merely represents the sexual weakness of all women, since ''tis as common / To err in frailty as to be a woman' – a clear echo of Hamlet's outraged exclamation, 'frailty, thy name is woman' (*Hamlet*, I.2.146).

Soranzo's verbal abuse is matched by his extravagant threats of violence: he will 'rip up' Annabella's heart to find the name of her lover, whom he will tear to pieces 'joint by joint' with his teeth. Her response is to laugh, eliciting a further threat that he will 'hew [her] flesh to shreds'. In the event, it is not Soranzo who rips up her heart, so his threats against her are thwarted. The image of the heart is prominent throughout this scene, together with that of blood, in a characteristic linking of love and violence. When Soranzo says 'Thus will I pull thy hair, and thus I'll drag / Thy lust-belepered body through the dust', most productions take 'thus' as an indication that he actually drags Annabella across the stage by her hair at this point, rather than as a threat of future violence, making us aware that he is not just engaging in verbal bluster, but is fully capable of carrying out all the violence he promises.

The powerful dramatic impact of this scene is created in a variety of ways, with a striking contrast between the raw passion and mutual recriminations of Soranzo and Annabella, and the cool ruthlessness of Vasques in wheedling out the truth from Putana. It is no surprise to see Soranzo emerge in his true colours here, since we already know the kind of man he is. It is something of a shock, though, to witness Annabella's transformation from the virtually silent, distressed compliance of her last few scenes into a scornful, defiant, almost hysterical recklessness. She openly expresses her contempt for Soranzo while praising the qualities of her secret lover, and she responds to his threats with laughter and singing. He is astonished at her reactions and his failure to instil fear into her – an astonishment brilliantly captured in a series of parallel questions: 'Dost thou laugh? […] Dost thou triumph? […] Dost thou not tremble yet?' Perhaps we are almost taken in by Soranzo's professions of love towards Annabella, 'I did too dearly love thee', which she affirms: 'I must confess, I know you loved me well.' However, he is merely responding to Vasques's advice that he should 'smother [his] revenge', and it is clear that his expressions of love are calculated and insincere, as Vasques acknowledges: 'This is well; / Follow this temper with some passion, be brief and moving: 'tis for the purpose.'

We have already seen Vasques's consummate skill in manipulating people in his dealings with Hippolita; now, he easily traps Putana into revealing the identity of Annabella's lover. We have seen his ruthlessness, too, in turning Hippolita's revenge upon herself, but his treatment of Putana still comes as a shock, and we may well wonder how he comes to have a gang of thugs at his command. It is interesting to speculate on Vasques's motivation. Loyalty to Soranzo clearly drives his actions, but he evidently enjoys his own manipulative skill and relishes the cruelty of a drawn-out, calculated revenge rather than the spontaneous violence that possesses his master. In the circumstances, his moral outrage at Annabella's incest seems entirely hypocritical. In his apparent honesty and his acting skill, Vasques has much in common with Iago in *Othello*, but while Iago works only for himself, Vasques, perhaps more interestingly, gains his sense of personal satisfaction from serving his master.

Act V scene 1

Annabella repents her sins and anticipates the tragic fate in store for her. The Friar, passing below her window, hears her repentance and agrees to deliver the letter she

has written to Giovanni, in her own blood, urging him also to repent, and warning him not to trust Soranzo's professions of friendship. She also expresses anxiety concerning the absence of Putana.

Annabella here consciously adopts the mantle of the tragic heroine, whose story, 'A wretched, woeful woman's tragedy', will stand as a warning to future ages. She acknowledges her 'lust' and her 'guilt', which will inevitably lead her to hell – 'The torment of an uncontrollèd flame!' – and submits herself to the dictates of her 'conscience'. Annabella's repentance seems sincere and deeply-felt, and follows on from the apparent submission she began to show towards Soranzo in the previous scene, but it is difficult to assess how the play judges her at this point, since in acknowledging her guilt she is effectively denying the validity of her love for Giovanni, expressed so forcefully earlier in the play. Shakespeare's Juliet, in contrast, never wavers in the strength of her love for Romeo, even after he kills her beloved cousin, Tybalt.

Annabella twice sums up her new-found moral awareness in the form of rhyming couplets, at lines 12–13 and 28–29. How we judge these, though, is problematic, since such couplets can be used in the drama of the period either to emphasise and strengthen a moral point, or to make it seem insincere or naïve, and Ford seems to employ them for both purposes during the play. Here, it is possible they indicate Annabella's attempts to convince herself that her conscience is prompting her in the right direction, while to the audience they suggest the inadequacy of summing up a profound moral issue in the form of a rhyming tag.

This scene illustrates the non-naturalistic flexibility of the early modern theatre. Annabella engages in soliloquy on the upper level; the Friar appears below, on the main stage, and overhears her. We do not need to imagine that Annabella is locked in her room and comes out on to her balcony, nor to provide a logical explanation of the Friar's presence in the street below. Equally, we do not have to consider the practicalities of Annabella's having written to Giovanni in her own blood, nor worry about how she planned to get the letter to him. Instead, the scene is governed purely by the needs of the drama, and the 'realistic' aspects of Annabella's situation are briskly accounted for in lines 48–55, before the scene is artificially rounded off with a double rhyming couplet.

One incidental point is worthy of note. At the end of IV.3, Giovanni visited Annabella and was directed by Vasques to her chamber. Ford neither tells us nor shows us what happened between them on that occasion. In the theatre, though, this is probably something we don't notice.

Act V scene 2

Vasques, having told Soranzo the identity of his wife's lover, goads him into action and helps him to plan his revenge, which is to be carried out at Soranzo's birthday feast.

Vasques's motivation is again interesting to consider in this scene. He seems to relish reminding Soranzo that his wife has cuckolded him, rubbing in the humiliation he must feel. It is as if Vasques revels in being the instrument of revenge and violence, and is worried that his master will let his 'pity' override his fury, avoiding the bloodshed that Vasques so eagerly anticipates. He seems to have misread Soranzo though, since, although his master promises to kiss Annabella and 'fold her gently' in his arms, this is clearly only for show, just as much as his instruction to Vasques to 'Entreat [...] gently' Giovanni and his father to the feast. We believe Soranzo when he claims to be 'as resolute / As thunder', renounces all ambition but revenge, and passionately concludes 'My blood's on fire!' The banditti, who were instrumental in the treatment meted out to Putana, are evidently in Soranzo's employment, ready to be called on when needed, and his intention that Annabella will be wearing 'all her bridal robes' will add a note of spiteful irony to his revenge.

Act V scene 3

Giovanni has unexpectedly discovered that he loves Annabella just as passionately even though she is married and, as the Friar arrives, he expresses contempt for his mentor's threats of eternal punishment. The Friar delivers Annabella's letter, but Giovanni does not believe its claim that their love has been discovered. Vasques brings Giovanni his invitation to Soranzo's birthday feast, which he accepts, rejecting the Friar's admonitions not to go. The Friar decides to return to Bologna, leaving Giovanni to plan a violent resolution of his story.

Giovanni's arrogance and his emotionally disturbed state combine to make him an unsympathetic figure in this scene. He is contemptuously dismissive of conventional social attitudes ('Busy opinion'); of Annabella's warnings ('low faint-hearted cowardice'); of the Friar's moral advice (the 'peevish chattering' of a 'weak old man'); of Vasques and the invitation he brings ('Sir, are you answered?'); and of his own prospects of eternal damnation ('Despair or tortures of a thousand hells, / All's one to me'). His continuing love for Annabella is expressed largely in physical rather than spiritual terms. Although he celebrates their 'two united hearts', he also talks about the 'taste of love', relishes the memory of the 'sweet and [...] delicious' kisses he 'reaped' from her before they first had sex, finds heavenly bliss, or 'Elysium', in 'A life of pleasure' and wonders if they themselves have somehow given away '[their] own delights'. 'Reaped' is a particularly interesting choice of verb, its implied violence suggesting the dominant sexuality of the male and, together with its associations with death (the Grim Reaper), anticipating the violent end he is planning for Annabella.

The Friar is clearly shocked by Giovanni's unrepentant emotional excess and recognises the 'bad, fearful end' that is closing in on his pupil. His deepest beliefs are attacked as 'slavish and fond [i.e. foolish] superstitious fear', and he himself accused of practising 'sorceries' masked as religion. Even his warnings about the dangers of Soranzo's plots are rejected, as his pupil openly plans 'To strike as deep in slaughter as they all'. Even so, there is something cowardly in the Friar's projected flight to Bologna in the face of this crisis. He cannot face up to witnessing Giovanni's fate ('I must not stay / To know thy fall'); his concern to 'shun this coming blow' could be interpreted as fear for

his own safety; and he abandons 'prayer' on behalf of his pupil, leaving him instead to 'despair'. Though all this may be seen as evidence of irresponsibility and cowardice, it also makes the Friar more human as he faces up to the inadequacy of his own beliefs, teachings and moral advice.

Act V scene 4

Vasques and Soranzo finalise arrangements with the banditti for their role in Soranzo's revenge. Vasques urges his master to be firm in his purpose and suggests that he should allow Giovanni access to Annabella; when Giovanni arrives, they send him to her room to hurry her along. Soranzo welcomes the Cardinal and the other guests to his birthday celebrations.

Careful staging is needed to ensure that the banditti, with their chorally spoken lines, are not comic figures. It is implied that they are not merely a gang of robbers, but banished men who are eager to return to society; hence the attractiveness of the offer of 'pardons' along with gold, so that they will subsequently be 'all free'. As Vasques says, their 'ends are profit and preferment' – which, in this context, means restoration to their positions in society.

It is interesting that Vasques still doubts Soranzo's determination, suggesting that he lacks 'a great mind' and urging him to remember his 'disgraces', his 'loss of honour' and the 'wrongs' he has suffered. Judging from his responses, Soranzo hardly needs his servant's encouragement, and the language of the scene is appropriately full of images of blood, vengeance and hellfire. Typically, it will not be enough merely to kill Giovanni; his life must instead be taken when he is fresh from his sinful lust, thus ensuring his instant and eternal damnation. This is why Giovanni is encouraged to visit Annabella in her chamber, ostensibly to 'get her forth', as she is 'scarcely ready yet' for the imminent birthday feast.

The Cardinal's presence at the feast is interesting. There is no love lost between him and Soranzo on account of the Cardinal's support of Grimaldi, Soranzo's rival. Perhaps Soranzo's intention in inviting him is to humiliate him with the bloody outcome of his revenge plot. The Cardinal's motives in attending are even more obscure, particularly in the uneasy company of Florio and Donado, whom he had treated with such contempt in III.9 after Bergetto's murder. Thus, the neutral stage direction, '*Enter* CARDINAL, FLORIO, DONADO, RICHARDETTO' and the courteous mutual flattery of the Cardinal and Soranzo's greetings, conceal a tense, edgy atmosphere, which needs to be emphasised in the staging. The scene is set for an explosive denouement.

Act V scene 5

In Annabella's chamber, Giovanni rebukes her for the apparent change in her feelings towards him and her resolution to be faithful to Soranzo. She is more concerned with the imminent fate Soranzo has in store for them, while he wonders if they will be reunited in the afterlife. Annabella urges Giovanni to escape while there is still time, but he has other plans and, after eliciting her forgiveness, stabs her. Giovanni exults in the fact that he has thwarted Soranzo's purposes, and removes Annabella's body.

The final encounter between brother and sister is tense, painful and moving. Their contrasting responses to the danger of their situation put them at cross-purposes. Giovanni is emotional, resentful, accusing, selfish and unyielding. Annabella is practical, realistic, loving and forgiving, though she ultimately accuses him of unnatural cruelty in killing her.

Though he has breached the moral and religious codes of his society, Giovanni proves himself to be a true child of its patriarchal structures: he assumes Annabella, as a woman, to be sexually frail and inconstant in her affections; he makes no attempt to discuss their situation with her on the basis of equality; he ignores her anxieties and her suggested course of action; and he gives her even less say in her fate than she had in her marriage choices. His arrogance continues to make him a singularly unattractive character, at his most contemptible in his accusation that Annabella has jilted him because Soranzo is better in bed:

> Hath your new sprightly lord
> Found out a trick in night-games more than we
> Could know in our simplicity? Ha, is't so?

Annabella takes this as a 'jest', or tactfully pretends to do so, and instead of standing up for herself against Giovanni's offensive allegations she is more concerned with his safety. She knows Soranzo is planning a violent revenge and has evidently not been taken in by his professions of love and forgiveness (see IV.3.117–46). She seems confused, though, about what course of action they should take: at first she advises him to 'be prepared to welcome' death, but later urges him to escape. In her anxiety, she is slow to realise what Giovanni intends to do, though when he talks of the 'Destinies' requiring her beauty back and her soul 'fill[ing] a throne / Of innocence and sanctity in heaven', she seems to grasp his meaning: 'Then I see your drift. / Ye blessed angels, guard me!' However, his kissing and talk of forgiveness apparently reassure her until he actually draws his dagger. Her first response is puzzlement: 'What means this?'; then she rebukes him, too late: 'O brother, by your hand?'; finally she forgives him, though still accusing him of being 'unkind'. She is, ultimately, an unwilling victim.

As throughout the play, the imagery of hearts and blood, fate and revenge is prevalent in this scene, pushing forward towards its violent climax. These key words are often supported by synonyms, as when Giovanni refers to Annabella's 'well-coloured veins'. At the end, Giovanni sees himself as an actor who has yet to perform his 'last and greater part'; though we might guess what that part will be – the role of revenger, perhaps, or tragic hero – nothing can prepare us for his next appearance.

Act V scene 6

As Soranzo's birthday feast begins, Giovanni enters with Annabella's heart on his dagger. He gives an account of the murder of his sister and of their incestuous relationship, provoking Florio to die of shock. Giovanni stabs Soranzo and fights with Vasques, who calls the banditti. They wound Giovanni and flee, leaving Soranzo and Giovanni to die in quick succession. Vasques explains his role in events to the Cardinal, and implicates Putana as an accessory in Giovanni and Annabella's incest. The Cardinal dispenses judgement, which includes Vasques's banishment and the appropriation by the church of all the money and property left by those who have died. Richardetto reveals his true identity, and the Cardinal passes a final judgement on Annabella.

This is an immensely challenging scene to stage, and any director will need to decide the extent to which laughter is a legitimate response to its gruesome events. When audiences laugh, as they often do at Giovanni's appearance with the heart on his dagger, it can be difficult to assess the reason for this. Is the laughter a defence mechanism to protect them from the horror of the scene? An acknowledgement of the play's descent into ludicrous melodrama? A recognition that the horror is entirely artificial, a mere stage spectacle? A sign of the audience's emotional immaturity? Or an indication that the moment has been incompetently staged?

Vasques's line 'What strange riddle's this?' is perhaps a clue to Ford's intentions, pointing to the emblematic significance of the spectacle rather than its literal reality. For Giovanni, as well as for the audience, his act has primarily symbolic significance, since the whole play has been centrally about the rivalry for possession of Annabella's heart, to which her brother here finally claims his right. Thus, the play's persistently reiterated imagery of hearts reaches its inevitable conclusion in this visualisation of Annabella's heart, and the word is used nine times in a variety of contexts in the first half of this scene. How far this interpretation helps a director to create the appropriate impact is a different matter, since audiences in Ford's time were likely to be much more alert to such emblematic spectacles than their modern counterparts, as well as being more open to a sense of generic ambiguity that can encompass shock and laughter, the horrific and the ludicrous, side by side.

Giovanni is no more sympathetic in this scene than elsewhere, and the play does not promote him as a tragic hero. There is no sense of self-knowledge, nor of his having learned anything as a result of his misguided passion for his sister, and he remains as arrogant and self-centred as he was at the beginning of the play. His language, though impressive, is essentially full of melodramatic exaggeration: 'The glory of my deed / Darkened the midday sun, made noon as night'; 'I digged for food / In a much richer mine than gold or stone'. Such metaphors imbue his actions, for himself, with a kind of false grandeur, but to his hearers, and the audience, they suggest only a kind of fearful madness. However, his dying speech has a more moving quality, and its homely metaphorical language – 'Death, thou art a guest long looked-for' – does suggest a greater degree of humility. His touching wish to see Annabella in the afterlife also, perhaps, elicits rather more sympathy for him than if he had died on his usual note of arrogant defiance.

Of the remaining characters in this final scene, the most worthy of comment is the Cardinal, who creates no more of a positive impression than he did earlier in the play. Like Giovanni's, his language strikes a note of melodrama – 'Incestuous villain!'; 'Speak, wretched villain, what incarnate fiend / Hath led thee on to this?' – which can arouse laughter in performance, probably deliberately. There is certainly something potentially comic in his urging of someone else to tackle Giovanni, 'Is none of you / Dares venture on him?', while he, presumably, hovers safely in the background; and also in the cowardice of his cry 'Raise up the city! We shall be murdered all!', just as Giovanni dies and the danger is patently over. Consequently, we view with irony the Cardinal's taking control in the final stages of the scene, and we can only respond to his apparently authoritative meting out of justice with some scepticism. When he condemns 'this woman' to be 'burnt to ashes', it is not clear whether he is referring to Annabella, who is indeed 'chief in these effects', or to Putana, whose role in events has just been outlined by Vasques. The demonstrative 'this' rather than 'that' is confusing, since it implies that the woman referred to is actually on stage. Perhaps there would be some dramatic value in having Annabella's mutilated body brought on by Vasques at line 60, thus more effectively precipitating Florio's death; or in bringing on the blinded Putana as Vasques speaks of her. In any case, the actor of the Cardinal needs to decide whom he is referring to, and his judgement is more cruel if it is the hapless Putana who is to be burned alive, rather than the already dead Annabella who is to be cremated – particularly in view of the lighter sentence of banishment given to Vasques. Vasques may well 'rejoice that a Spaniard outwent an Italian in revenge' – another line that usually gains a laugh in performance.

If the Cardinal's moral status were not already equivocal, his confiscation of 'all the gold and jewels' left by Florio and Soranzo 'to the Pope's proper use' confirms our comic contempt for him and for the corrupt Church that he serves. He is caught off guard by Richardetto's sudden revelation of his true identity, which has all the comic bathos of anticlimax, since we have probably forgotten all about him. Thus, by the time the Cardinal speaks the play's final couplet, he has lost what little moral authority he had, so that it is impossible to accept unquestioningly his judgement on Annabella; when he asks 'Who could not say, 'Tis pity she's a whore?' we must provide our own answer, rather than accepting the implied moral closure of his rhetorical question. We may, perhaps, share the pity without sharing the condemnation.

Characters and characterisation

One of the most common errors made by students is to write about characters in literature as if they were real people. In reality, they are linguistic constructs created to fulfil a range of purposes in different texts. While an assessment of the 'personality' of a fictional or dramatic character may be a valid part of literary analysis, it is much more relevant to examine characterisation — the techniques a writer uses to create particular characters for particular purposes. When it comes to a play, the 'text' belonging to each character is a blueprint for interpretation by different actors, and one important aspect of analysis is to consider the range of potential performances that a text makes available.

Modern readers and audiences often look for psychological consistency in the portrayal of character, but this concept would have been alien to Ford and his contemporaries. Characters function at each moment in a play script according to the dramatic needs of that moment, and while there may often be a clear sense of consistency or development, characters in Renaissance drama are equally often contradictory and ambiguous. An illusion of coherence can be created in performance by the fact that a single actor is playing the role, and the overall effect is often to suggest the inconsistency and complexity of real people.

Characters in a play are defined through language and action. What they do, what they say, how they say it, and what other characters say about them determine the response of a reader, while on stage these techniques of characterisation are enhanced by costume, gesture, facial expression and other performance features. In examining the text, you need to be sensitive to the characters' use of verse or prose, the rhetorical and figurative qualities of their speech, the imagery they use and that associated with them, and the tone of their language. Characters who are given soliloquies are placed in a privileged position in relation to the members of the audience, who are allowed to share their innermost thoughts.

The notes that follow offer some general pointers to approaching the characters in 'Tis Pity She's a Whore; a more detailed response has already been offered in the scene summaries and commentary section (pages 21–48), which you should use in conjunction with this section.

Giovanni

Giovanni is a young man in the grip of an obsession, whose self-absorption and arrogance remove from him the sympathy that we might accord to a more conventional tragic hero. However, an actor in the role must also make us aware of him as the 'miracle of wit' and 'wonder of [his] age' described by the Friar:

> How did the university applaud
> Thy government, behaviour, learning, speech,
> Sweetness, and all that could make up a man! (I.1.50–52)

Giovanni must also be physically attractive enough to justify Annabella's description of him as having the 'blessèd shape / Of some celestial creature' (I.2.127–28).

The opening scene establishes Giovanni's essential qualities: his passion for Annabella, with its emphasis on lust (he demands to know why his 'joys' should be 'ever banished from her bed' (I.1.37)); his emotional torment, or 'burdened soul' (I.1.13); his self-centred arrogance, with the words 'I', 'myself', 'me' and 'my' constantly on his lips; his reliance on logical reasoning rather than moral precepts to argue the case for his feelings and actions; and his willingness to challenge the very basis of Christian faith if he cannot get his own way, concluding the scene with the declaration that he will abandon his allegiance to God to follow what he sees as his destiny: 'I'll swear my fate's my God' (I.1.84).

As the plot develops, Giovanni diverges little from these initial impressions. As he himself confesses in soliloquy when we next see him, 'I'm still the same' (I.2.153), despite his professed attempts to follow the Friar's advice to pray and repent, which he characterises as 'old men's tales / To fright unsteady youth' (I.2.152–53). He adopts the tone and language of a conventional romantic lover in building up to his confession of his feelings for Annabella, but we also see his potential for violence when he offers her his dagger and urges her to 'Rip up [his] bosom' to inspect his very heart (I.2.205–06). He is also selfishly dishonest, deceiving her with an outright lie in telling her that the Church has sanctioned their love (I.2.236–37).

Following their love-making, Giovanni is teasingly affectionate in mocking the loss of Annabella's virginity, but strikes an ominous note in his realistic acknowledgement of the pressure on his sister to marry, eliciting her promise to be faithful to him. He seems to delight in confessing to the Friar that he and Annabella have consummated their love, reverting to logical reasoning in his justification, and indulging in elaborately poetic praise of her qualities (see II.5.12–26, 49–58). Temporarily, he seems to have escaped from the emotional torment that consumed him at the start of the play, gaining a brief moment of happiness and fulfilment. When he spies on Soranzo's wooing of Annabella, his confidence in her love for him is confirmed, but her sudden illness throws everything into confusion. On learning that Annabella is pregnant, Giovanni remains outwardly in control, enlisting Putana's help in keeping away their father and the Doctor, sending comfort and encouragement to his sister, and fetching the Friar to advise her and, if the worst comes to the worst, 'absolve her' (III.4.30).

In the face of Annabella's marriage to Soranzo, however, Giovanni is reduced to sulking and sullenness — understandably so, but making him into a graceless, unsympathetic figure. His assertion that he would 'dare confusion / And stand the horror of ten thousand deaths' (IV.1.17–18) rather than have seen Annabella in another's arms comes across as petulant melodrama, as does his dismissal of Vasques and his refusal to toast the married couple (IV.1.19–20, 27–28). He is given no response to Hippolita's ill-fated disruption of the wedding feast, and disappears from the play for four scenes, apart from a brief appearance to visit his sister (IV.3.239–50) in an encounter we are not shown. Perhaps Ford is saving him up for his climactic role in Act V.

In his next major scene, Giovanni switches from the height of elation, or what he calls 'the jubilee / Of my retired delights' (V.3.17–18), prompted by his continued enjoyment of Annabella's love, to the depths of disbelieving despair, when he reads the letter written in her blood, in which she reveals that their relationship has been discovered. His bad-tempered acceptance of the invitation Vasques brings to Soranzo's birthday feast is typical of his petulant immaturity, but his subsequent vow to turn events towards a bloody conclusion reveals a mind frighteningly out of control. Acknowledging that the Friar is right about Soranzo's vengeful intentions, he swears 'To strike as deep in slaughter as they all' (V.3.62), promising that, if he is to suffer 'a glorious death', he will ensure that 'with me they all shall perish' (V.3.76, 79). Powerful as his language is here, it still creates the impression of melodramatic immaturity rather than tragic stature, and it is not surprising that the Friar finally chooses to give up on his pupil.

In his encounter with Annabella, Giovanni continues to forfeit our sympathy, as he chastises her for her 'treacherous' and 'faithless' determination to be 'honest' to her husband, which he jealously puts down to Soranzo's more varied sexual skills (V.5.1–15). His language becomes more powerfully tragic as he builds up to killing her, but it is an essentially selfish act, dictated by the abstract qualities of 'Revenge' and 'honour' (V.5.86), and his disruption of the feast with her heart on his dagger is the ultimate demonstration of possession, proving publicly that he, and only he, has had Annabella's heart throughout the play: 'nine months I lived / A happy monarch of her heart and her' (V.6.44–45). His shocking act is all about himself: he refers to 'the glory of my deed' (V.6.21) and calls himself 'a most glorious executioner' (V.6.33), and in his dying line he appropriates Annabella as his possession as he wishes, in the afterlife, 'Freely to view my Annabella's face' (V.6.107). In essence, there is little difference between the Giovanni of the first scene and the last.

Annabella

Annabella's role offers more variety for an actor than Giovanni's. Oddly, this is partly because she is largely confined to reacting to events rather than initiating them, and there are a great many contrasting pressures on her that lead to a diverse range of responses. Unlike Giovanni, she at first keeps her feelings suppressed: having observed the quarrel between two of her suitors, Soranzo and Grimaldi, she counters Putana's enthusiastic speculation with the revealing admission:

> But tut'ress, such a life gives no content
> To me: my thoughts are fixed on other ends.   (I.2.67–68)

What these ends might be is revealed when, having dismissed her third suitor, Bergetto, as an 'idiot' (I.2.118), she spies the 'blessèd shape / Of some celestial creature' (I.2.127–28), which Putana identifies as her brother. Her sympathy with his 'woeful' demeanour is powerfully expressed, building to an ominous climax, 'My soul is full of heaviness and fear' (I.2.132–39). At first she resists his expressions of love for her: 'If this be true, 'twere fitter I were dead' (I.2.215); but she soon confesses that she has for a long time thought about him in the same way: 'what thou hast urged, / My captive heart had long ago resolved' (I.2.240–41). Already, her heart is in Giovanni's possession, as it is, literally, at the end of the play.

After their love-making, she responds with modest embarrassment to his teasing, but expresses a strong determination never to marry. She lives up to her promise in her firm but sympathetic rejection of Bergetto, leading his uncle to comment 'Why, here's plain dealing; I commend thee for't' (II.6.54). However, she has a harder time with Soranzo, and in her witty, sarcastic responses (III.2.15–42) we see a new side of her. She makes a mistake, though, in promising Soranzo that if she must marry, it will be to him, leaving herself open to the consequences of her unforeseen pregnancy and the practical decisions and social pressures that immediately ensue. Her interview with the Friar shows both her distress and her apparent penitence; she is a 'Wretched creature' (III.6.6). However, her agreement to marry Soranzo seems motivated more by the fear of eternal torment in hell, so vividly described by the Friar (III.6.7–30) than by genuine repentance. She says little in this scene, allowing her fate to be controlled by the patriarchal demands of religion and family. She is largely silent, too, at the wedding celebrations that culminate in Hippolita's gruesome death, and an actor in the role must decide on her demeanour throughout these events. Clearly, her limited response, 'It is a fearful sight' (IV.1.99), conceals a turmoil of suppressed emotions.

However, Annabella breaks free from her role of silent victim in confronting Soranzo's violent fury when he has discovered her pregnancy. Her responses are both courageous and foolhardy: she insults him, calling him a 'Beastly man' (IV.3.15), and admits she married him 'not for love / […] but for honour' (IV.3.22–23); yet she is also conciliatory, recognising his 'over-loving' nature (IV.3.17) and promising that, if he showed patience, she would 'see whether [she] could love [him]' (IV.3.25). Tact eludes her, though, as she showers elaborate praise on her unnamed lover — 'So angel-like, so glorious', in contrast to the husband who is 'not worthy once to name / His name without true worship' (IV.3.36–42). She veers towards hysteria as she laughs and sings in the face of Soranzo's increasingly violent threats (IV.3.53–63), but when he becomes more loving and conciliatory after Vasques's intervention, she too softens, confessing to him that his 'words wound deeper than [his] sword could do' (IV.3.129), kneeling for forgiveness and going obediently to her room. This is a varied and complex emotional scene for Annabella and is one of the highlights of her role.

When we next see her, Annabella is confined to her room and reflecting on her situation in soliloquy, casting herself as the conscience-stricken protagonist in a 'wretched, woeful woman's tragedy' (V.1.8). Though she partly blames Giovanni for her sad fate, at the same time she wishes she could save him from his share of divine punishment. The letter she sends to him via the Friar, who has conveniently overheard her repentance, is written in her own blood — presumably indicating that she has been denied writing materials. In it, she urges him to repent too, but warns him of the danger he is in from Soranzo's plotting. 'Now I can welcome death', she concludes (V.1.59), though when she faces it in her next scene she is distressed that it comes at the hand of her brother. At first, she begs him not to 'waste / These precious hours in vain and useless speech' (V.5.18–19), since Soranzo's banquet is a 'harbinger of death' which he, like her, should 'be prepared to welcome' (V.5.27–29). Soon, though, she is urging him to escape. When she senses his intention to kill her, her readiness for death seems to desert her — while she is perfectly prepared to meet her death at the bidding of Soranzo, she is not expecting it from her brother and lover: 'O brother, by your hand? [...] Brother, unkind, unkind' (V.5.87–93). Throughout this scene, Annabella is touchingly human and contradictory, in contrast to the single-minded obsessiveness of her brother. Her death is both shocking and moving.

Florio

Florio is a wealthy citizen of Parma, a proud and loving father who is anxious to arrange a socially advantageous match for his daughter — though he is emphatic in asserting to Donado that he 'will not force [her] 'gainst her will', his 'care [being] how to match her to her liking', and concluding, 'I would not have her marry wealth, but love' (I.3.3–11). It is clear, however, that he himself favours Soranzo (see II.6.122 and III.2.1–6). Giovanni is evidently a source of worry to him, since his academic studies seem to be affecting his health (I.3.5–6). Florio's authority is evident in his handling of the disturbance outside his house (I.2.21–26) and in the firmness with which he rebukes Soranzo for his part in it (I.2.52–62), and it is also evident that he enjoys playing the host, as he invites his guests back in for wine. Generally, though, Florio's concerns are touchingly domestic: he is pleased to find Annabella at her needlework (II.1.51), proud of her musical skills (II.1.74–75) and anxious about her health (II.1.54–56). He is tactful and sensitive in handling Bergetto's wooing of Annabella, but can also be firm with her in insisting she read Bergetto's letter (II.6.27) and give him some kind of answer (II.6.42–44). Although he is surprised she doesn't have her mother's ring about her (II.6.36–39), he does not make an issue of it, and he is happy to remain on friendly terms with Donado despite Annabella's rejection of Bergetto's suit.

When Annabella falls ill, however, Florio's decision to marry her speedily to Soranzo seems unwise, though he is careful to act with the backing of the Friar. Following Bergetto's murder, Florio remains a sympathetic friend to Donado, but his own authority is weakened in the face of the Cardinal's arrogant inflexibility and it is made clear that his social standing, as a businessman rather than a member of the nobility, puts him in a subservient position. His furious anger is powerfully expressed — 'Justice is fled to heaven and comes no nearer' — but he is forced to acknowledge that 'Great men may do their wills, we must obey', taking comfort in the eventual judgement of Heaven (III.9.62–69). Perhaps he takes his own advice to Donado to 'drown [his] cares in wine' (IV.1.22); at any event, he says little during his daughter's violently disrupted wedding banquet and disappears from the play until Soranzo's even more horrifically disrupted birthday feast, the shock of which kills him. Florio is in many ways a sympathetic character; Ford draws in him a convincing portrait of an ordinary man, proud of his family and his social position, enjoying the rewards of a successful business life, but ultimately destroyed by his children's tragic passion.

Putana

Putana is in many ways a much coarser version of Juliet's Nurse, and there is nothing in the play that seems to support her rather odd designation as Annabella's 'tutoress'. In Italian, her name meant strumpet or whore, and her characteristics seem as appropriate to such a description as they are inappropriate to her role as governess to the daughter of a respectable household. She repeatedly addresses Annabella as her 'charge', suggesting the responsibility she has for her, but in their first scene this responsibility seems to consist entirely of offering opinions and advice in relation to Annabella's suitors, mostly couched in lewd and bawdy innuendo. She herself sees her tutoring in these terms, commenting 'I hope I have tutored you better' in suggesting that Annabella should not be interested in the simpleton Bergetto just because he brings his uncle's money with him (I.2.119–26). Though Annabella finds Putana's ceaseless chatter irritating in this scene (see I.2.69, 73, 84, 99), it is evident that there is an affectionate relationship between them, and Annabella is clearly distressed and anxious when she is deprived by Soranzo of Putana's company in the later stages of the play (see V.1.49–50, V.5.24).

Putana is an unfit guardian for Annabella, however. Her moral irresponsibility and preoccupation with sex lead her to encourage Annabella's incest, keeping it secret only to avoid scandal (II.1.41–48). Her hypocrisy is evident in the way she elicits money from Donado by telling him she has been encouraging Annabella to think positively of Bergetto (II.6.14–20). She is thrown into a panic when Annabella falls pregnant, partly fearing for her own exposure: 'O sir, we are all undone, quite undone, utterly undone, and shamed forever!' (III.3.1–2).

In her commendable distress at Soranzo's harsh treatment of his wife, she easily falls victim to Vasques's cunning, revealing the identity of Annabella's lover partly to gain 'everlasting love and preferment' for herself from Soranzo (IV.3.202). Her reward, though, is cruelly disproportionate to her offences, as she is carried off by Vasques's thugs to confinement in the coal-house where her eyes are to be put out and her nose slit if she screams (IV.3.230–32). Her ultimate fate is uncertain. If, as seems likely, she is the 'woman, chief in these effects' referred to by the Cardinal (V.6.132), she is sentenced to be burned alive. It is possible, though, that the Cardinal is talking about the dead Annabella; this point would have to be clarified in a production. Putana is, at any rate, harshly punished for her complicity in incest and adultery.

Friar Bonaventura

The Friar is Giovanni's tutor and confessor, whose admiration for his young protégé has led him 'Rather to leave [his] books than part with [him]' (I.1.54). His shock and outrage at Giovanni's confession of incestuous feelings towards his sister are framed in the conventional language of sin, lust, death and hellfire, but there is also a sense in which the Friar feels let down by the pupil he has esteemed so highly, who misuses his skill in rational argument to justify his sinful thoughts. He urges Giovanni to embrace repentance, employing memorably powerful language, but promises that, if his desires persist, he will 'think on remedy' (I.1.80). The Friar is, of course, bound by the confidentiality of the confessional, but we are led to question his advice and behaviour as events unfold. He could, for example, have insisted on seeing Giovanni and Annabella together, and urged them to reveal the truth to their father, instead of merely relying on the power of moral and religious exhortations. Instead, he finds himself drawn into increasingly dubious advice and involves himself inextricably in the complications of their situation.

The Friar's hellfire sermon to Annabella (III.6.7–30) seems to have the desired effect on her, but his advocacy of marriage to Soranzo 'for [her] honour's safety' and 'to save [her] soul' (III.6.36–37) is dangerous and ill-advised, paying no heed to Soranzo's violent nature and previous sexual history, nor to Giovanni's likely reaction. His smooth-tongued officiating at the marriage smacks of both hypocrisy and naïvety as he wishes prosperity to the 'happy couple' (IV.1.6), and it is notable that he remains silent and inactive throughout the subsequent enactment of Hippolita's misfired revenge, merely commenting at the end, with somewhat ludicrous understatement, 'that marriage seldom's good, /Where the bride-banquet so begins in blood' (IV.1.107–08).

There is no evidence that the Friar subsequently seeks to remedy his misguided actions by offering solace to Annabella; fortuitously, he overhears her repentance while passing beneath her window, perhaps being most pleased to hear her refer to him as 'that blessèd friar' (V.1.24), and agrees to deliver her blood-inscribed letter to Giovanni. When he finds Giovanni still celebrating his incest, 'the jubilee / Of [his] retired delights' (V.3.17–18), and fails to persuade him to escape the danger he is in, his only recourse is to abandon his charges in what must be seen as an act of moral cowardice, fleeing to Bologna 'to shun this coming blow' and 'leave [Giovanni] to despair' (V.3.66–70). In retrospect, Florio's greeting to the Friar as 'one /That still bring blessing to the place you come to' (III.4.24–25) must be read with a certain amount of irony.

Soranzo

Soranzo is a nobleman whose interest in marrying Annabella, presumably on account of the dowry she will bring with her from her rich father, is compromised by his own sexual history. His adulterous affair with Hippolita is well known (see Putana's comments at I.2.91–94), and we have no reason not to trust Hippolita's own account that he had sworn to marry her in the event of her husband's death but went back on his word after she had contrived to bring about her widowhood (see II.2.68–82). His response, that his vows were 'wicked and unlawful' (II.2.86) and that he repents his implicit part in her husband's demise, shows blatant hypocrisy, and his treatment of Hippolita is uncompromisingly harsh:

> Learn to repent and die; for by my honour
> I hate thee and thy lust. You have been too foul.   (II.2.99–100)

In view of Soranzo's past, it seems surprising that Florio sees him as a suitable match for his daughter even if, as he believes, Annabella prefers him over her other suitors (see I.2.52–54). It is certainly clear that Florio disapproves of Soranzo's aggressive response to Grimaldi's disparaging remarks about him, which has led to the brawl that disrupts his hospitality at the start of I.2. Soranzo's arrogance is evident in his explanation that he has ordered Vasques to 'correct [Grimaldi's] tongue, / Holding a man so base no match for me' (I.2.42–43).

Arrogant, aggressive, revengeful, adulterous, unfaithful, hypocritical: Soranzo's qualities do not bode well for his proposed marriage to Annabella; yet he also reveals an unexpected vein of romanticism as we find him alone in his room reading love poetry and revising it to suit his own apparent feelings for Annabella. There are various ironies in this. Soranzo finds Sannazar's poem unduly cynical in its analysis of the 'pain', 'unrest' and 'disdain' of love, altering it to express love's sweetness, 'pleasures' and 'joys' (II.2.1–11). It is the former qualities that he himself is to experience, however, both in Hippolita's immediate intrusion on his reflections and in his subsequent marriage to Annabella. Soranzo, at any rate, is an unlikely exponent of courtly love poetry, and his romantic notions are soon dispelled in his uneasy interview with Annabella: ''Tis plain, she laughs at me!' (III.2.39). Not unnaturally, when a betrothal is hastily patched up in response to Annabella's illness, he is anxious for reassurance: 'Lady, say you so too?' (III.6.53). Revealingly, though, he views their marriage in terms of a successful merchant venture: she is the 'most precious jewel', the 'prize' that has 'enriched [his] life' (IV.1.9–10). When Hippolita intrudes on the wedding feast, Soranzo at first responds with restraint, perhaps through gritted teeth: 'You have too much engaged us. […] Hippolita, I thank you' (IV.1.55–62); but at the revelation of her revenge plot and her gruesome death he merely comments approvingly on Vasques's service and calmly leads his new wife home, thanking 'the heavens for this escape' (IV.1.100–04).

The next time we see Soranzo, it is in his true colours, responding to his discovery of his wife's illicit pregnancy with physical violence and verbal abuse. His anger is understandable and, unlike the jealous husbands in many other plays of the period, he has good cause for his passion. His behaviour, though, is excessive, and we feel that he would be perfectly capable of carrying out his threats: 'I'll rip up thy heart';

'I'll hew thy flesh to shreds' (IV.3.53, 58). His violence is demonstrated as he presumably drags her across the stage by her hair (IV.3.60–61), his present action indicated by the repetition of 'thus'. Only Vasques has the capacity to calm his rage, but his apparently conciliatory behaviour is merely a mask that conceals his burning desire for 'swift revenge' (IV.3.150). This revenge is pursued with intense determination through the remainder of the play, and Soranzo's true nature is demonstrated in the fact that he seems to have a gang of thugs or 'banditti' at his disposal, whose members are enlisted in his plotting of Giovanni's death. Vasques considers his master potentially weak, however, and feels the need to 'edge [his] resolution' (V.4.20), after which he can safely say to Soranzo, 'Now you begin to turn Italian!' (V.4.28) — in other words, he is living up to the national stereotype of hot-headed vengefulness. When Giovanni out-manoeuvres him, he is furious — 'Shall I be forestalled?' (V.6.15); he is forced to hand over the fulfilment of his revenge to Vasques as he himself suffers an ignominious public death at his own birthday celebrations.

Vasques

For an actor, the role of Vasques is perhaps the most rewarding in the play. His combination of wit, cynicism, intelligence, cruelty, Machiavellian cunning and consummate acting ability make him a perversely attractive character, in a similar vein to Shakespeare's Iago or Richard III. Vasques is a Spaniard who was taken into the service of Soranzo's father in childhood and has continued to serve the son with loyalty and dedication (see V.6.115–19). Even Hippolita acknowledges his loyalty, while persuading him that it will go unrewarded (II.2.126–28, 135–36), and he himself twice takes pride in the fact that he has 'paid the duty to the son which [he] vowed to the father' (V.6.111–12, also 138–39). His loyal service encompasses plotting and scheming, fighting duels on his master's behalf, and acting as spy, torturer and organiser of contract killings. Perhaps these activities match his own predilections, for as Donado says to him, 'You are ever forward / In seconding contentions' (I.2.28–29). His length of service to Soranzo's family suggests that he is not a young man, which is confirmed by his references to his 'grey hairs' (I.2.6) and his 'old years' (II.2.145). His nature is summed up in his final words, 'I rejoice that a Spaniard outwent an Italian in revenge' (V.6.145–46), though this seems a rather optimistic interpretation of the backfired revenge plot in which his master has perished. In view of his central role in the play's violent events, he escapes lightly by being condemned only to banishment.

First seen beating Grimaldi in physical combat, with accompanying insults, Vasques soon proves himself equally adept in more subtle and devious skills of manipulation, giving him the quality of a typical stage machiavel. He is skilful in gaining the confidence of both Hippolita and Putana, and pretends effectively to be the agent of reconciliation between Soranzo and Annabella; he is, indeed, effective in calming his master's anger, but only so that he can relish a more carefully plotted revenge. Vasques habitually views things in terms of theatre and performance: he comments, for example, that Soranzo's 'part has been scurvily played' (II.2.101) and promises to be 'a special actor' in Hippolita's revenge plot (II.2.156). More specifically, he acts as the presenter of Hippolita's masque (IV.1.30–33); directs Soranzo's performance for Annabella's benefit ('Follow this temper with some passion, be brief and moving', IV.3.115); guarantees that the banditti will play their roles effectively ('I will undertake for their parts', V.4.2); and instructs them in their cue ('You know the watchword, till which be spoken, move not', V.4.13–14).

Though Vasques seems motivated entirely by loyalty to his master, he never-theless revels in his own craftiness and cruelty. In the feigned support and comfort he offers to Hippolita, Annabella and Putana, his prose style acquires an exagger-ated sympathy and moral outrage: 'Now the gods forfend! [...] Alas poor lady [...] Sir, you must be ruled by your reason and not by your fury: that were unhuman and beastly' (IV.3.78–85). This is a tone he uses principally in his seductive manipula-tion of the female characters, but when they have served his purpose his language loses all pretence of decorum: 'I'll help your old gums, you toad-bellied bitch!' (IV.3.229–30). He is perversely gleeful in discovering the worst — 'Why, this is excellent and above expectation! Her own brother? O horrible!' (IV.3.233–34) — since it gives him even more scope to relish thoughts of violent retribution and to 'tutor [Soranzo] better in his points of vengeance' (IV.3.236–37). Though we may enjoy Vasques's resourceful wit, we can only be appalled by his sadistic cruelty.

Grimaldi

Grimaldi's status, as both a nobleman and a soldier, is questioned by Soranzo and Vasques. Soranzo accuses him of 'A lowness in [his] mind', even though he may be 'equal in [his] blood', concluding that 'a man so base' is unworthy of being fought with in person (I.2.37–43). He is also sarcastic about his military background, calling him a 'gentleman, whom fame reports a soldier /(For else I know not)' (I.2.31–32). Vasques, too, gives his soldierly qualities short shrift (I.2.4–6) and calls him a 'poor shadow of a soldier' (I.2.10–11) — and he easily overcomes Grimaldi in physical combat. Grimaldi himself seems particularly sensitive to his status and reputation, and contemptuous of others. He is, in fact, closely related to the Duke of Monferrato, and hopes his connections will win him Annabella's love (see II.3.28–33); even so, he is gullible enough to consider using love potions on her (II.3.39–41), until Richardetto embroils him instead in his plot against Soranzo. Though he recognises his plan to kill Soranzo as 'an unnoble act, [which] not becomes /A soldier's valour', he concludes that such 'policy' is the only way to his desire (III.5.2–5). When he kills Bergetto by mistake, he takes refuge in the protection of his powerful connections, and from the safety of sanctuary with the Cardinal he can afford to sound humble and apologetic (III.9.40–51). Having fulfilled his function in the plot and incidentally thrown light on the Church's corruption, Grimaldi disappears from the play.

Donado

Donado is a wealthy businessman and friend of Florio. He is an authoritative figure, shown in his reprimanding of Vasques for brawling in the street (I.2.27–29), and his status is acknowledged in the grim task the Cardinal charges him with at the end of the play (V.6.132–37). He is a sympathetic character, refreshingly human in both his affection and his frustration towards his nephew, the latter summed up in his exasperated phrase, 'This is intolerable' (I.3.65). Contemplating Bergetto's inadequacy as a wooer, he touchingly reflects on his own youth: 'When I was young/ I could have done't, i'faith' (I.3.25–26), but more often his nephew's childish stupidity reduces him to sarcasm and insults. He exaggerates to Annabella Bergetto's feelings towards her (II.6.6–10), but bears no grudge when she rejects him, commending her 'plain dealing' and promising continued friendship with Florio (II.6.54–57). His grief when Bergetto is murdered is genuine and moving, and his anger at the Cardinal's protection of Grimaldi represents one of the play's most powerful moments: 'Is this a churchman's voice? Dwells Justice here?' (III.9.62). Donado remains an important background figure in the play, giving instructions for the removal of Hippolita's body (IV.1.105) and, despite his earlier anger, accepting his role in the Cardinal's disposition of justice.

Bergetto

Bergetto, as his uncle admits, is nothing but a 'great baby' (I.3.46), an engaging simpleton who is more interested in the latest fairground attractions than in his own marriage prospects. Confident of his own merits, he breezes through the world in search of pleasure and satisfaction in the company of his loyal servant, Poggio. Bergetto is an innocent abroad, as gullibly ignorant of fairground scams as he is of the traditional formalities of love-making. He is keen to stand on his own two feet, insisting on writing and delivering his own love letter, and disobeys his uncle's instructions to stay at home and keep out of trouble. When Poggio suggests the result will be a 'whipping', he stands on his dignity: 'Dost take me for a child, Poggio?' (II.4.44–45). Set upon and beaten in the street, he laughs at his attacker until he realises he is injured, at which point his laughter turns to tears. He is taken in and looked after by Richardetto and Philotis, who immediately replaces Annabella in his affections — something he tells Annabella with no trace of tact and no hint of embarrassment: 'By this light, she had a face methinks worth twenty of you, Mistress Annabella' (II.6.90–91). Bergetto's proposed elopement with Philotis confirms his sense of independence, and her modest affection towards him, encouraged by her uncle, enhances the audience's sympathetic view of him. His sexual naïvety, though, is emphasised in his response to the erection provoked by his kissing her (III.5.45–46).

Ford employs Bergetto for a number of dramatic purposes. He emphasises Annabella's restricted choice of marriage partners, and he introduces a comic strain into the play, relieving the emotional intensity of the principal characters. However, the dramatist has a dramatic shock up his sleeve in subjecting this likeable buffoon to a violent death — a death which disconcerts the audience by first being treated comically, in the language Bergetto himself uses to describe his wounds and his pain, before invoking a genuinely tragic response, notably in Poggio's moving lament for his master's death (III.7.37). Shakespeare had done something similar with the death of Mercutio in *Romeo and Juliet*, the difference being that Mercutio is an intelligent, complex, tortured character for whom a violent death seems somehow more dramatically fitting. Bergetto's death is both more shocking and more inconsequential, having little direct effect on the subsequent progress of the plot.

Poggio

On the face of it, Poggio is a loyal and affectionate servant to Bergetto, and their relationship forms an interesting contrast to that of Soranzo and Vasques. However, there is scope for an alternative interpretation of Poggio's role. He is clever and witty, often adding bawdy remarks to his dialogue with Bergetto (as at II.6.65), and the suggestiveness of Bergetto's letter to Annabella is presumably due to Poggio's 'advice' (see II.4.16–32). Sometimes, Poggio is supportive of his master, such as when he tells Donado that it would be 'very unhealthy' for Bergetto to stay indoors (II.4.40). However, some of his comments could be played sarcastically, suggesting a certain contempt for Bergetto, as in their first appearance (I.2.103–17); and at one point he deliberately fails to help him out with his ready wit: 'Answer for yourself, master' (I.3.48). He encourages Bergetto in his elopement with Philotis, presenting it in the light of an act of rebellion against his uncle (III.1.1–7).

However the role is played, though, there can be no doubting the depth and sincerity of Poggio's grief at Bergetto's death, expressed in the simplest of language: 'How! Dead? [...] O my master, my master, my master!' (III.7.34–37). In view of this, some directors have been dissatisfied with Poggio's restricted role in the follow-up scene, III.9, in which Ford limits him to knocking at the Cardinal's gate, and have added various kinds of business to demonstrate his grief and anger; two examples are given in the commentary on this scene on page 38.

Hippolita

We first learn of Hippolita as 'the lusty widow' who Putana mentions as having had an adulterous relationship with Soranzo (I.2.92–94), and we hear most of her story from her own mouth as she reminds her former lover of how he treated her. According to her story, Soranzo's emotional and sexual conquest of her succeeded against her better judgement, and he swore to marry her in the event of her husband's death. Hippolita encouraged her husband to take a dangerous journey, during which he apparently died, but Soranzo went back on his promise and added insult to injury by transferring his hopes of marriage to Annabella, referred to contemptuously by

Hippolita as 'Madam Merchant' (II.2.48). Hippolita passionately presents herself as the wronged woman, apparently consumed by guilt for her part in her husband's death, though it was only her 'advice' (II.2.81) that took him into danger. In reality, Hippolita is motivated by jealousy and the desire for revenge, and the power of these feelings blinds her into misreading the character of Vasques, foolishly enlisting him in her revenge plot by offering herself to him in marriage: he will be 'lord of me and mine estate' (II.2.150). As a result, her plot, aiming to poison Soranzo while he is feasting with his new bride, spectacularly misfires. Double-crossed by Vasques, she dies in agony, venting her blood-curdling curses on the newlyweds and their progeny. This is an apt conclusion to her role, which, with its exaggerated and passionate language, has verged on melodrama throughout.

Richardetto

The details of Richardetto's history are sketchy and unclear. He evidently knew of his wife's adultery with Soranzo, the 'disgrace' of which, according to her, hastened his death (II.2.39). We know that she urged him to undertake a dangerous journey from Parma to Leghorn to bring home his recently orphaned niece, and that he 'caused it to be rumoured out' that he had died on the way (II.3.10). He has now returned to Parma with his niece Philotis, disguised as a doctor, ostensibly to observe the 'scope' of Hippolita's 'loose adultery' (II.3.12) but actually, as Philotis fears, to pursue 'some strange revenge' (II.3.15). A testimonial to Richardetto's character comes from the unlikely source of Soranzo, who calls him:

> So noble in his quality, condition,
> Learning, behaviour, entertainment, love,
> As Parma could not show a braver man.   (II.2.92–94)

Admittedly, Soranzo's intention is to increase Hippolita's guilt, but there must be some truth in this encomium or it would be pointless. However, the Richardetto we see in the play hardly lives up to this description, and his calculated revenge plot, using Grimaldi as the agent of Soranzo's murder, equates him morally with those who have wronged him. He makes a convincing doctor, persuasively diagnosing Annabella's symptoms, but he is an irresponsible uncle and guardian to Philotis. It is not clear why he encourages her relationship with Bergetto, and he never acknowledges his culpability in the latter's death, instead disposing of his niece hastily into a nunnery — perhaps to avoid her incriminating him. He witnesses his wife's humiliating and gruesome death with apparent equanimity, joining in with the general feeling that she has got what she deserves: 'Heaven, thou art righteous' (IV.1.86), though he later confesses that she has 'paid too soon / The forfeit of her modesty and life' (IV.2.2–3). His sense of the divine justice meted out to 'lust and pride' (IV.1.99) grows into the feeling that he need no longer pursue his revenge against Soranzo since 'there is one / Above begins to work' (IV.2.8–9), and he determines merely to remain in Parma to observe 'the end of these extremes' (IV.2.19). Richardetto's language, in contrast to his wife's melodramatic passion, is flat, colourless and factual, rising only occasionally to vivid imagery that underlines his emotional state: 'I'll laugh and hug revenge' (III.5.22). He fades into the background, again silently observing the appalling events of the final scene before, in a somewhat absurd anticlimax, revealing his true identity to the surviving dignitaries (V.6.151–55), whose muted response is entirely understandable.

Philotis

Philotis may seem to be an ineffectual character, passively obedient to her uncle's will, but there is scope for an actor in the role to give her rather more spirit. She is astute enough to perceive Richardetto's revengeful motives (II.3.14–15) and, though he urges her affections towards Bergetto, there is evidence that her feelings develop independently of his influence, notably in her response to Bergetto's kiss (III.5.37). Her grief at her lover's death is expressed with a moving simplicity, though in few words, and her shocked reaction to Richardetto's decision to place her in a nunnery shows a momentary independence, soon stifled (IV.2.22). Her final couplet in the play (IV.2.29–30) is sad and touching, and she takes her place in the dramatic structure as a striking contrast to the other three female characters.

The Cardinal

Though he only appears three times, the Cardinal's role in the play is crucial to its impact, setting its shocking events in the social and political context of a corrupt and hypocritical Roman Catholic Church — a frequent target of Protestant English Renaissance drama. Far from promoting justice or showing compassion, the Cardinal is interested only in maintaining power and influence through his political alliances; he takes Grimaldi into his protection because of his links with the Duke of Monferrato, stressing that the murderer is 'nobly born / Of princes' blood' even though Florio thought him 'too mean a husband' for Annabella (III.9.56–58) — though there is no evidence in the play for this assertion. The Cardinal speaks with brusque arrogance, complaining about the clamour at his door, showing a callous disregard for Bergetto's death and for the feelings of his grieving uncle, and concluding with two dismissive commands: 'Learn more wit [...] / Bury your dead' (III.9.60–61). As often as not, he talks of himself in the royal plural, and behaves with patronising superiority when Soranzo welcomes him to his birthday feast (V.4.51–60). His shock and outrage at the events and revelations of the final scene seem merely conventional, his apparent compassion for Florio's death (V.6.61–63) hypocritical in the light of his previous contempt for him, and his cowardice is almost comic: 'Is none of you / Dares venture on him?' (V.6.63–64) — an effect that can be heightened in performance if he is cowering in the background. When all seems safe, he assumes authority as of right and disposes apparently random justice, allowing Vasques to escape with his life and ensuring that Soranzo's and Florio's wealth and property are appropriated by the Church, in a speech (V.6.148–50) that invariably gets a big laugh in the theatre. Through this presentation of the Cardinal, Ford ensures that his final judgement on Annabella, and thus the play's title, can only be viewed ironically, inviting us to make our own alternative assessment of her character and her story.

Minor characters

Various smaller roles in the play help to give the sense of a richly detailed social panorama; in other respects they are largely functional. The **officers** who are summoned after Bergetto's death are deferential towards Florio, of whose affairs they seem to know something, but fearful of the Cardinal's power and unwilling to venture on to his property. The **banditti** employed by Soranzo and Vasques to do their dirty work are presumably banished men who relish the promise of money accompanied by a free pardon (see V.4.5–11). In the text, they always speak in unison; this can have a comic effect in performance, and a modern director will probably handle their lines differently. For their killing of Giovanni, they appear masked, giving them a more sinister quality. The final scene also calls for non-speaking **attendants**, presumably to serve food and drink and clear away the bodies at the end. Oddly, no attendants are specified at the wedding feast (IV.1), which does, however, require a number of **ladies** to take part in Hippolita's masque. The **Cardinal's servant** has one offstage line. These minor roles could be covered by about six actors, perhaps including those playing Grimaldi and Philotis. In the original production, the officers probably doubled with the banditti, and the ladies (played by boys, of course) with the attendants.

Language and style

Some linguistic difficulties

Language is not a fixed entity with a stable and immutable system of configuration and usage. New words are created, old ones become redundant, while others change their meaning. Four hundred years is a long time in the life of a language, so it is hardly surprising that we find considerable differences between the language of a Renaissance play and that of today. The 'rules' of modern English spelling, punctuation, grammar and syntax were not really established until the eighteenth century, and in Ford's time language was much more flexible. Frequently we find evidence of a language in flux, with archaic and modern usages working side by side.

The impact of such changes on our understanding of the language of Renaissance drama is often exaggerated, however, and our difficulties with it are sometimes self-fulfilling — we expect it to be difficult, so we find it so. When we listen to the plays spoken by skilful actors, we understand parts that seemed obscure on the page. We may not grasp the meaning of every word, with all its subtleties of nuance and implication, but we follow the story, understand the characters and their relationships, and appreciate the ideas behind the play. The point about Shakespeare made in the RSC's 2003 programmes is equally valid for Ford: 'it is up to us, his audience, not to sit on each line with a dictionary but to become caught up in the live experience of theatre.'

Sometimes, the difficulties in Renaissance drama do not reside in the language at all, but in the wealth of classical allusions or historical references that lie outside the frame of our own limited general knowledge. Or perhaps we are confronted by alien value systems or unfamiliar social structures that challenge our understanding. Often, though, it can be the metaphorical richness of the dramatic language that puzzles us, overwhelming us with figurative images at one remove from what is being described or the feelings that are being expressed. However, Ford's language is poetry, and we should accept it as such. In responding to poetry, we are required to open our own imaginations to the mysterious power of words to make us see things afresh, from an unlikely angle or a startling perspective. 'Understanding' does not have to be limited to working out a literal meaning; it can be intuitive, imaginative or emotional. The language of poetry enriches us.

Verse and prose

Verse is language that is organised rhythmically according to particular patterns of metre and the arrangement of lines. In plays of Ford's time and earlier, verse was the conventional medium of dramatic discourse. Plays were not regarded as naturalistic slices of life, and the heightened language of verse was felt to be appropriate to their non-realistic status as performance texts. However, dramatists increasingly varied the range of their dramatic language to include speeches and scenes in prose, the language of everyday speech and writing. Verse tended to be given to noble and royal characters, expressing romantic or elevated feelings, while prose was generally used by characters of lower social status, for comic or domestic scenes, for letters read out loud, or to indicate mental disturbance.

Verse

By Ford's time, one particular verse metre had come to dominate the language of plays. This was based on a line of ten syllables, arranged so that the beats, or stresses, fell on every second syllable. Thus, each line consisted of five units (or metrical feet), each consisting of an unstressed syllable followed by a stressed one, as follows:

$$\sim\ /\quad \sim\ /\quad \sim\ /\quad \sim\ /\quad \sim\ /$$

Each of these units is called an iambic foot, and since there are five of them in each line, the metre is called iambic pentameter. Here are two examples from the play:

```
     ~    /    ~    /    ~     /    ~      /    ~    /
I will | not force | my daugh | ter 'gainst | her will          (I.3.3)
      ~     /    ~     /    ~    /     ~      /    ~   /
'Tis boot | less now | to show | yourself | a child             (III.9.1)
```

In the earlier drama of the time, such as Shakespeare's first plays, the rhythms of iambic pentameter tended to be kept very regular, at the risk of becoming monotonous. As dramatic verse developed, it became more flexible, incorporating an increasing number of irregularities. Two of the most common variations on the basic iambic pentameter are as follows:

(1) An eleventh, unstressed syllable added to a line, giving what is called a feminine ending:

```
    ~ /  ~ /    ~     /    ~    /    ~   /    ~
As ev | er you | would have | me know | you loved | me          (III.2.60)
    ~    /    ~    /    ~   /    ~   /    ~   /    ~
For this | offence | I here | receive | Grimal | di             (III.9.54)
```

(2) Reversing the stress on the first foot of a line, so that it begins with greater emphasis:

```
   /    ~    ~   /    ~   /    ~   /     ~   /
Holding | a man | so base | no match | for me                   (I.2.43)
   /    ~    ~    /    ~    /    ~  /    ~    /
Come to | her, tell | him she's | recov | ered well             (III.3.26)
```

Sometimes both variations occur in the same line:

```
    /    ~     ~    /     ~   /   ~   /    ~   /   ~
Pleasures | farewell, | and all | ye thrift | less min | utes    (V.1.1)
    / ~    ~     /    ~  /   ~  /    ~   /    ~
Bury | your dead. | Away, | Grimal | di; leave | 'em            (III.9.61)
```

In passages of dialogue, one verse line can be shared by two speakers. Most editions make this clear by the way the text is set out:

SORANZO   Tell me his name!

ANNABELLA   Alas, alas, there's all.
               Will you believe?

SORANZO   What?

ANNABELLA   You shall never know.

                                                        (IV.3.50–51)

Again, in early plays, each verse line tended to be a unit of meaning. Later dramatists much more frequently ran the sense of one line into the next, a technique called enjambement; they also created more heavy breaks in the middle of a line, known as caesuras. Both of these have the effect of obscuring rather than emphasising the underlying rhythm of the lines. Although Ford's verse is generally fairly regular, the following speech of Hippolita illustrates the effectiveness of enjambement and caesura, together with reversed stresses, repetition and alliteration, in capturing the character's physical and emotional anguish:

> O, 'tis true,
> I feel my minute coming. Had that slave
> Kept promise — O, my torment! — thou this hour
> Hadst died, Soranzo. —Heat above hell-fire! —
> Yet ere I pass away — cruel, cruel flames! —
> Take here my curse amongst you: may thy bed
> Of marriage be a rack unto thy heart. —
> Burn, blood, and boil in vengeance! O my heart,
> My flame's intolerable! — May'st thou live
> To father bastards, may her womb bring forth
> Monsters, and die together in your sins,
> Hated, scorned and unpitied! — O — O! (IV.1.87–97)

Rhyme

The standard verse form of the play, like most plays of the period, is blank verse, which simply means iambic pentameter with no rhyming. However, Ford, like many of his contemporaries, uses rhyming verse to create particular effects. In *'Tis Pity*, there are frequent rhyming couplets embedded in the text of the play. These are often used at the end of scenes, or to round off key speeches, giving an effect of closure or finality. The first scene, for example, ends on a double rhyming couplet, in which both the Friar and Giovanni confirm their slightly different strategies for dealing with the latter's incestuous feelings (I.1.81–84). At other times, rhyming couplets are used to highlight particular moments, either to emphasise them or, on occasions, to make them sound insincere. In the first encounter between Giovanni and Annabella, for instance, it is worth considering the impact of the couplets, which occur at the following points: I.2.195–98 (N.B. 'those' rhymes with 'lascivious'), 223–24 ('destiny' rhymes with 'I must die'), 230–33, 257–58. It is also interesting that this scene does not conclude with a couplet — perhaps because Giovanni and Annabella's relationship, far from reaching closure, has only just begun.

Rhyming couplets can suggest powerful emotion (III.9.66–69), melodrama (II.2.104–05, III.8.18–19), moralising (IV.1.107–08), determination (V.5.106–07); or they can alert us to view the speaker in an ironic light, as with the closing couplet of the play (V.6.158–59).

If you are writing about the verse of the play or analysing a speech in verse, you need to beware: do not just describe the features of the verse, but analyse and comment on the effects it creates in the lines you are looking at. For example:

- How do regular, fluid verse rhythms create different effects from irregular, broken ones?
- How might an actor respond to the particular features of the verse in developing his or her character?
- What is different about the way the verse is used by different characters, or by the same characters at different times in the play?
- How does the verse work with other language techniques to create the particular effect of a speech?

Prose

Most Renaissance plays contain sections in prose as well as verse, and *'Tis Pity She's a Whore* is no exception. As already indicated, prose tended to be given to characters of lower social status, and was used in comic or domestic scenes, for the reading aloud of letters, or to indicate mental disturbance.

These categories of prose use do not always apply, however, and it is important to establish the particular effects of prose speeches and scenes in the structure of the play as a whole, especially when prose and verse are mingled as freely as they are in this play.

It is a mistake to think that prose is somehow more naturalistic or realistic than verse. Prose can encompass the language of novels, textbooks, newspapers, magazines, letters, diaries and legal documents, and it can be as structured and artificial as verse. It is the everyday language, in speech and writing, of people of varying degrees of education and literacy, and is consequently infinitely varied in its rhythms, grammatical structures and vocabulary. In *'Tis Pity She's a Whore*, there are four main characters, in addition to the officer and the banditti, who always speak in prose. The use of prose by Vasques, Putana, Bergetto and Poggio marks them out as either servants or comic characters or both.

Sometimes other characters, whose normal mode of discourse is verse, are given prose when they are in conversation with these characters, as when Grimaldi is arguing with Vasques (I.2.1–20, 44–50), Hippolita and Vasques are plotting together (II.2.106–46), Giovanni converses with Putana (III.3.1–19) or Vasques (IV.3.242–50), and on virtually every occasion when Donado is talking to his nephew.

Occasionally, there are other snatches of dialogue in verse scenes that do not have the quality of regular verse and seem instead to be in prose. For example, the opening of Giovanni and Annabella's first encounter (I.2.159–86), although containing odd verse lines, consists essentially of brief prose exchanges, suggesting the characters' initial hesitant uncertainty. As they gain confidence, however, the scene moves into regular blank verse, heightened further by a number of rhyming couplets. This scene demonstrates Ford's flexibility in his mingling of prose and verse discourse in the play.

When you are considering Ford's use of prose, you need to ask a number of questions, such as:

- What kinds of characters are speaking, and in what context?
- Do these characters use prose throughout the play? If not, why do they use it here?
- What precedes or follows each prose section? Does the prose have the effect of lowering the dramatic temperature after a verse scene? Does it heighten the impact of a verse scene that follows? Or does it simply provide a contrast of tone?
- What kind of prose is it? Is it elaborate, courtly and artificial or uneducated, colloquial and comic? Does it employ long, complex, balanced sentences or short, straightforward ones? What linguistic devices does it employ, and what effects do these create?
- What possibilities for interpretation by the actors are presented by the particular qualities of a prose speech?

Imagery

An *image* is a mental picture conjured up by a particular word or phrase. When writers use related patterns or clusters of images, they are using *imagery* as a literary technique. Such imagery may serve a number of purposes: it may be a feature of characterisation, infusing characters with particular associations; it may contribute to the creation of mood and atmosphere; or it may support the thematic significance of the text. Ford's use of imagery in *'Tis Pity She's a Whore* is subtle and pervasive. Among the notable image clusters, the following are of particular interest and significance:

- love
- lust
- death
- blood
- the heart
- blushing

- fate, fortune and destiny
- revenge (or vengeance)
- honour
- justice
- hell and hellfire
- time

When we watch and listen to a performance of the play, we are probably not consciously aware of such verbal patterning, but it will nevertheless help to condition our response. Furthermore, aspects of the imagery are likely to have been taken into account in the design and staging of the production, so that set and costumes, lighting, music and sound effects may well enhance the play's linguistic features. Closer reading and study of the text reveals some of these verbal features in more detail, enabling us to assess their impact at a more consciously analytical level. In writing about imagery, it is therefore important not merely to note image patterns, but to consider the effects they create on our response to the play.

Many of the images listed above are abstract qualities, drawing attention directly to the play's themes, and to the moral and intellectual debate in which the characters are often engaged. Others are more visceral in their impact, strongly suggestive of the physicality of human beings, such as the heart that pumps blood around the body but can be ripped out (see I.2.205–06 and IV.3.53). This image culminates in the physical action of the play's bloody climax, but also carries moral resonances in the sense of shame that suffuses the cheeks with blood, as in Annabella's blushes after consummating her love for her brother (II.1.1–8). 'Do not blush', urges Giovanni, claiming that Annabella has 'inflamed /A heart whose tribute is [her] brother's life'. She denies that there is 'a modest crimson' printed on her cheeks, since it is her 'heart's delight' that has prevailed with her sexually. This short passage demonstrates both the suggestiveness and the subtlety of Ford's imagery, linking the heart with related ideas in a web of physical, emotional and moral associations. Tracking such key images through the play is a revealing and rewarding exercise.

Structure

'Tis Pity She's a Whore was first staged at the indoor Phoenix Theatre, and its five-act structure partly reflects the need for regular breaks to trim the candles that illuminated the stage and auditorium. Ford carefully uses the five acts to develop the progress of the action.

Act I kicks off the main plot, introducing the incestuous attraction between brother and sister and setting it in the context of Annabella's unwanted suitors. Grimaldi's resentment against Soranzo is established, and Bergetto is developed as a likeable idiot.

Act II sets Giovanni and Annabella's now-consummated relationship against the first stages of the subplot of Hippolita's revenge on Soranzo, introducing Richardetto and his niece to complicate matters. We are carefully reminded of Grimaldi's projected revenge, while Bergetto's rejection by Annabella gives way to his infatuation with Philotis. A number of plot strands are now ripe for further development.

In Act III, we see Soranzo's unsuccessful wooing of Annabella reversed when she falls pregnant, culminating in their betrothal. While Hippolita's revenge plot simmers in the background, that of Grimaldi and Richardetto reaches a climax in the mistaken killing of Bergetto, building up to Donado and Florio's angry confrontation with the Cardinal, vainly demanding justice. In modern productions, this is where the single interval is usually taken.

Act IV plunges us straight into Soranzo and Annabella's wedding celebrations and their melodramatic disruption by Hippolita's misfired revenge and her gruesome death. Richardetto and Philotis fade from the action, and the focus narrows to the marital conflicts of Soranzo and Annabella, fired by his discovery of her pregnant state. Vasques tutors Soranzo in revenge, and the downward spiral of violence is marked by his appalling treatment of Putana. The act ends on a downbeat note as the unknowing Giovanni arrives to visit his sister.

Act V maintains the same tight focus, juxtaposing the preparations for Soranzo's revenge with the progress of Giovanni's counterplot, and building remorselessly from Annabella's house arrest to her violent death and the climactic bloodbath. Ford manages the pacing and climax of this sequence, as of the whole play, with consummate skill.

Working alongside the play's five-act structure are other markers of its architectural unity. For example, the various revenge plots and their progress offer one way of viewing the narrative development, while the three disrupted feasts, in I.2, IV.1 and V.6, provide a different, more emblematic kind of structural coherence. Looked at another way, there is an interesting two-part division in which all the subplots and subsidiary characters are removed by IV.2, leaving the remainder of the play to focus on the working out of the central relationships of Giovanni, Annabella and Soranzo. An alternative two-part structure might be seen through the presence of the Cardinal at the play's most powerfully climactic moments. Far from cancelling each other out, all these structural patterns contribute to the sense of a carefully crafted drama.

Themes

The themes of a literary text may or may not have been developed consciously by the author. Usually, we have no means of knowing an author's intentions; what is important is the impact of the text on a reader or, in the case of a play, an audience. Even if an author has written explicitly about the thematic content of a work, that does not preclude other themes from coming to the attention of particular readers. It can even happen that a text unconsciously undermines its author's professed themes: in *Moll Flanders*, for example, Daniel Defoe seems to relish the sexual immorality he is ostensibly attacking, while in *To Kill a Mockingbird*, Harper Lee's portrayal of the black characters sometimes employs elements of the very racial stereotyping that the novel aims to expose.

Responding to the themes of a complex drama such as *'Tis Pity She's a Whore* is not as simple as asking what the 'moral' of the play is. The themes range across personal relationships, social structures, religious and political morality and philosophical reflections on the meaning of life; they are developed through a web of overlapping and interconnecting ideas and are made evident through plot and narrative, characterisation, language and imagery.

Incest

Incest is one of the few remaining taboos of Western culture, and is almost as shocking to us now as it would have been for early seventeenth-century audiences. When the Channel 4 television soap, *Brookside*, presented an incestuous relationship between brother and sister in the early 1990s, there were outraged responses, and cases of incest reported in the media arouse revulsion and disgust. That Ford makes such a relationship central to his play is often cited as evidence of the decadence and corruption of Jacobean and Caroline theatre.

Looking at the way Ford deals with the subject, though, it is perhaps misleading to consider incest as a 'theme' of the play. Instead, it is better regarded as the mainspring of the plot, merely a variation on the 'blocking' device that separates the lovers — a dramatic feature represented in *Romeo and Juliet* by the feud between the Montagues and Capulets, in *Othello* by the protagonists' differences in age and race, or in *The Winter's Tale* by the supposed discrepancy in social class between Florizel and Perdita. The play does not exactly offer a discussion of incest in abstract moral terms. However, by presenting a comparatively sympathetic view of the lovers, particularly Annabella; by promoting a critical view of the society in which they live; and by suggesting a condemnatory attitude to church hypocrisy, Ford avoids a clear denunciation of incest and, by extension, might therefore seem to be condoning it. However, there are no records of the play having aroused controversy when it was first staged, and it seems likely that it was felt appropriate for performance at the court of Charles I some time between 1629 and 1633.

'Tis Pity was not the first play to investigate incestuous relationships, though it was the first to place incest at the centre of the plot and treat it so explicitly. Modern readers and viewers of *Hamlet* often detect hints of incest in the play's subtext, both between Hamlet and his mother, Gertrude, and between Laertes and his sister, Ophelia; Webster's *The Duchess of Malfi* makes Ferdinand's opposition to his sister's remarriage explicable partly in terms of his implicitly incestuous feelings towards her; and Middleton's *Women Beware Women* presents a young girl, Isabella, cynically tricked into an incestuous relationship with her uncle. In none of these plays, though, is incest the principal focus of attention.

For modern readers and audiences, the play's apparent avoidance of a moral viewpoint on incest often seems baffling. The Friar's horrified condemnation of the sibling lovers and his terrifying picture of the eternal torment meted out to those who have 'dreamt out whole years in lawless sheets /And secret incests' (III.6.25–26) seem melodramatic, and clearly do not represent the voice of the play as a whole, while the final judgements of the Cardinal, characterising Giovanni as an 'Incestuous villain' (V.6.51) and Annabella as a 'whore' (V.6.159) are undermined by his own blatant hypocrisy. We are left to draw our own moral conclusions and to reflect, perhaps, that the force of love is simply no respecter of the barriers imposed by society, religion or family relationships. Those who are caught up in its power despite such barriers possibly deserve, in a more sincere way than the Cardinal expresses it, our 'pity' (V.6.159).

Revenge

Revenge is clearly a central motif in *'Tis Pity She's a Whore*, and the number of active revengers escalates as the plot unfolds. The fight between Grimaldi and Vasques at the start of I.2 has apparently originated in Soranzo's desire for revenge on Grimaldi for making disparaging remarks about him to Annabella (see I.2.30–43). Grimaldi, in his turn, vows revenge on Soranzo (I.2.47). Subsequently, we meet Hippolita, determined to enact revenge on Soranzo for abandoning her. For the first time, the emotional charge transmitted by the act of revenge is made explicit: 'Revenge shall sweeten what my griefs have tasted' (II.2.161). Almost immediately, we learn that Hippolita's supposedly dead husband, Richardetto, still lives, nursing his own 'strange revenge' (II.3.15) against Hippolita and Soranzo, and soon allying himself with Grimaldi. He provides the poison with which Soranzo is to be killed at Grimaldi's hand, but the play's language is by now suggesting the melodramatic quality revengers often acquire, emphasised by the rhyming couplet that registers his gloating anticipation:

> Thus shall the fates decree,
> By me Soranzo falls, that ruined me.   (II.3.62–63)

The effect of such language is to make the characters seem obsessed, diminishing any empathy we may have with them and removing from them the humanity that more naturalistic dialogue imparts. Richardetto continues in this gloating, melodramatic vein — 'So, if this hit, I'll laugh and hug revenge' (III.5.22) — personifying revenge as an independent entity. This is something that perhaps derives from one of the earliest revenge plays, Kyd's *The Spanish Tragedy*, in which Revenge actually appears as a character, presenting for the dead Andrea the cycle of revenge that follows his murder.

However, Richardetto's and Grimaldi's joint revenge plot misfires, mistakenly falling on the harmless Bergetto. There is an implicit suggestion here that revenge rebounds on the innocent, and the moral impact on the two revengers is worth noting. Grimaldi seeks the protection of his powerful friends, expressing sorrow for Bergetto's death but remaining defiant in justifying his intention of murdering Soranzo (see III.9.40–51). The Cardinal, notably, offers no condemnation of his motives. Richardetto's response is complicated by the fact that he also witnesses his wife's revenge against Soranzo go horribly wrong, again embodied in the language of melodrama: 'Burn, blood, and boil in vengeance!' (IV.1.93). He is chastened, and although he sees that 'vengeance hover[s]' over Soranzo (IV.2.4), he determines to let it run its own course. He retreats into religious conviction: 'there is one / Above begins to work' (IV.2.8–9) — reflecting the biblical dictum, 'avenge not yourselves […]: Vengeance is mine; I will repay, saith the Lord' (*Romans*, 12.19). In urging his niece to enter a nunnery, Richardetto is partly demonstrating awareness of his own wrongdoing as abortive revenger, asking for her 'hourly prayers' for her 'poor unhappy uncle' (IV.2.23–24). It is interesting that the less socially exalted characters, Florio and Donado, do not seek revenge for Bergetto's death and the Cardinal's intransigence. Instead, they demand 'justice' and, concluding that it has 'fled to heaven', they accept that they must 'obey' the wills of great men and trust that 'Heaven will judge them for't another day' (III.9.63–69).

At this point in the play, it seems that the revenge plots have burned themselves out, with an implicit moral condemnation of vengeance as a motive for violence. However, with Soranzo's discovery of his new wife's pregnancy, we are immediately plunged into a further spiral of revenge and counter-revenge. Soranzo claims that he 'will not slack [his] vengeance' (IV.3.76), while Annabella, though welcoming death, promises to 'leave revenge behind' for him to feel (IV.3.71) — presumably assuming Giovanni will avenge her. Vasques advises Soranzo to 'smother' his revenge (IV.3.98), arguing against his master's desire for 'swift revenge' (IV.3.150) and persuading him that 'Delay in vengeance gives a heavier blow' (IV.3.162). Once again, it is the emotional satisfaction of revenge that is emphasised here. Delay causes frustration too, though; Soranzo complains that his 'soul / Runs circular in sorrow for revenge!' (IV.3.256–57), which is 'all the ambition' to which he aspires, since his 'blood's on fire!' (V.2.25). By the time he is assuring the banditti that what they do 'Is noble and an act of brave revenge' (V.4.9), the audience is in a position to make quite a different moral judgement.

Soranzo's revenge is ultimately forestalled by Giovanni. As we view with horror the play's final bloodbath, the words 'revenge' and 'vengeance' ring increasingly hollow, and their link with 'honour' is revealed as mere equivocation. When Giovanni proclaims, in killing Annabella, 'Revenge is mine; honour doth love command' (V.5.86), we can only marvel at the cruelty of his moral delusion, and when he reiterates the sentiment in stabbing Soranzo, 'Now brave revenge is mine' (V.6.74), the adjective is again exposed as a lie. Revenge is not brave.

Soranzo fulfils his revenge, but the play views his achievement with irony. Rejoicing that he has 'lived / To see [his] wrongs revenged on that black devil' (V.6.89–90) he almost immediately dies, with Giovanni still alive — surely a moment that might elicit the audience's scornful laughter. The play's final comment on revenge is an even more explicitly comic line, when Vasques rejoices that he, 'a Spaniard', 'outwent an Italian in revenge' (V.6.145–46). Without making any explicit moral comment on revenge, as he does in his other tragedy, *The Broken Heart*, where 'Revenge proves its own executioner' (*The Broken Heart*, V.2.147), Ford has powerfully demonstrated that revenge merely corrupts and destroys all it touches, including the revenger himself, and those who espouse it are worthy of our contemptuous laughter.

Social class

When Hippolita refers slightingly to Annabella as 'Madam Merchant' (II.2.48), she is expressing the class contempt of the aristocrat for the burgeoning middle classes, whose money came from business and trade rather than from inherited wealth. In this case, why should Soranzo, a nobleman, desire Annabella's hand in marriage? Merchants like Florio were often extremely wealthy, and the dowries they supplied as part of their daughters' marriage settlements were exceedingly tempting to impoverished aristocrats whose accumulated assets were often stretched to the limits by the expense of maintaining their country houses and estates, as well as the demands of debt, perhaps incurred by gambling or other manifestations of a lavish lifestyle, or by state taxation such as that Charles I regularly attempted to impose on his better-off subjects. Thus, while Soranzo gets a boost to his finances, Florio gets the thrill of his family's social elevation. As Friar Lawrence says to Capulet in *Romeo and Juliet*, referring to Capulet's choice of Count Paris as his daughter's intended husband, 'The most you sought was her promotion' (*Romeo and Juliet*, IV.4.98). It clearly makes Soranzo feel better to imagine himself romantically attached to Annabella, demonstrated by his absorption in Sannazaro's love poetry at the start of II.2.

There is a clear distinction in the play between the aristocrats, Soranzo, Hippolita, Richardetto and the Cardinal, and the merchant families of Florio and Donado — something that needs to be emphasised through costume, speech and body language in productions of the play. Although there is clearly social interaction between the two classes, there is also an underlying reservoir of snobbery and resentment. This even extends to the servant classes, with Vasques considering himself superior not just to Putana, but even to Grimaldi, claiming to him that Soranzo 'keeps servants thy betters in quality and performance' (I.2.11–12) — presumably meaning himself. Grimaldi's social status is, in fact, ambiguous. Described in the list of characters as 'a Roman gentleman', he is apparently related to 'the Duke of Monferrato' (I.2.76) and, according to the Cardinal, is 'nobly born / Of princes' blood', even though Florio supposedly 'Thought him too mean a husband' for Annabella (III.9.56–58). The Cardinal's treatment of Florio and Donado demonstrates his class prejudice and class solidarity most nakedly: despite knowing of their grief at Bergetto's murder, he refers to them as 'saucy mates' who are not fit to be his guests (III.9.29–31).

Ford makes no explicit comment on issues of social class, but it is notable that the play's nobility are the ones engaged in violence and revenge, and whose power enables them to impose hypocritical moral judgements as well as arbitrary justice. The quiet dignity of Donado and Florio is in striking contrast. As 'ordinary' citizens of Parma, they are models of hospitality and responsibility, bearing no grudges (see II.6.54–57) and harbouring no thoughts of revenge. Revealingly, the play's final, hypocritical moral judgements belong to the aristocrats, with Donado's attempted intervention cut off mid-line (V.6.155), though with a patronising assurance of friendship from Richardetto. The implied criticism of the privileged and powerful must have been particularly telling when the play was performed for Charles I and his court, as it probably was between 1629 and 1633.

Religion

The play features two ministers of the Catholic Church, a Friar and a Cardinal, both of whom are found wanting. However, it is not simply an attack on Roman

Catholicism, though many of its early audiences may well have viewed it in this way. Leading Protestant clergymen of Ford's time were figures just as controversial as the play's Cardinal: Bishop Laud, for example, later Archbishop of Canterbury, was bound up in the operation of political power, and espoused controversial modes of Anglican worship. It must have seemed to many that the Protestant Church demonstrated as much of a conflict between true spirituality and worldly concerns as any representative of the despised Catholic faith portrayed on stage.

The Cardinal is the easier of the two figures to dismiss. Power resides with him at the play's two climaxes, and in making his judgements he is seen to lack compassion, acting only according to class solidarity and financial considerations, while throwing in the odd moral judgement. Since the Cardinal twice refers to the Pope (III.9.53, V.6.150), he is made by Ford to represent the whole of the Catholic hierarchy, rather than being a mere aberration. His idea of 'justice' (III.9.53) is to offer the Church's protection to a murderer; for Donado and Florio this simply demonstrates that 'Justice is fled to heaven', which will ultimately judge the Cardinal and all other 'Great men' who behave like him (III.9.63–69). What the play fails to offer, though, is any sense that such a heaven actually exists. At the end of the play, the Cardinal's moral assessment of Annabella, following almost immediately on his appropriation of 'all the gold and jewels' left by Florio and Soranzo 'to the Pope's proper use' (V.6.148–50), merely shows his cynical hypocrisy.

Friar Bonaventura is a different matter. On the face of it, he seems to wield the play's moral authority, but he operates in secret, bound by the confidentiality of the confessional — an aspect of Catholic practice much criticised by Protestants — and he works largely by instilling fear in those who have transgressed, rather than by offering more positive moral and spiritual guidance. His hellfire sermon to Annabella is certainly effective, but it is unable to prevent the ensuing tragedy, and the play seems to question his terrifying vision of eternal damnation. Although he follows up his lecture by asserting to Annabella that 'Heaven is merciful, / And offers grace even now', he seems just as concerned for her 'honour's safety' as for the saving of her 'soul' (III.6.34–38). His urging of her to marry Soranzo proves a disastrous miscalculation, and heaven's 'grace' is conspicuously absent from the consequences — again suggesting the absence of any such heaven. The Friar seems to be flailing around in conventional moral and religious pieties that are totally ineffective in the real world of human relationships, and as often as not he seems to be protecting himself as hypocritically as the Cardinal. His blessings on the 'happy couple', Soranzo and Annabella, have a hollow ring in the circumstances (IV.1.6), and his reason for ultimately abandoning his responsibility towards Giovanni and Annabella is weak and cowardly:

> I must not stay
> To know thy fall: back to Bologna I
> With speed will haste, and shun this coming blow.   (V.3.65–67)

He is indeed spared from seeing the dreadful consequences of his pastoral failure, and from accepting his own partial responsibility for them.

The religious theme of the play does not reside exclusively in these two characters, however. Richardetto acquires a level of spiritual awareness during the events of Acts I–III, largely through witnessing the violent consequences of revenge in the deaths of Bergetto and Hippolita. He becomes convinced that divine justice has begun to operate — 'there is one / Above begins to work' (IV.2.8–9) — and that 'No life is blessèd but the way to heaven' (IV.2.21). Whether the play shares his religious optimism is not clear, since it leads him to urge his niece to enter a nunnery — largely, it seems, so that she can remember him in her 'hourly prayers' (IV.2.23). Philotis's response is crucial to our understanding of the religious dimension of the play. If she seems reluctant, as her initial question suggests — 'Uncle, shall I resolve to be a nun?' (IV.2.22) — then her farewell to the 'world, and worldly thoughts' and her yielding to 'chaste vows' (IV.2.29–30) will seem like another enforced moral choice imposed on a woman by her male mentor for his own peace of mind. If Philotis delivers her three lines with enthusiastic commitment, however, then perhaps we may be more inclined to see genuine moral and spiritual forces existing behind the hypocrisy and weakness of the play's official representatives of Christian faith. As with the other themes of the play, Ford offers no explicit answers.

The play in performance

Early productions

'Tis Pity She's a Whore was first performed at the Phoenix (or Cockpit) Theatre by Queen Henrietta's Men, and may well have been performed at court. There are few records of these early performances, though Thomas Ellice reports that he witnessed the play 'With admiration' in his Commendatory Verse to the first published edition in 1633, and a note at the end of the printed text speaks of 'The general commendation deserved by the actors in their presentment of this tragedy'. The play remained in the theatre's repertoire for ten years or so, which suggests that it was popular enough to continue making money, and it was revived when the theatres were reopened after the restoration of Charles II in 1660. Samuel Pepys saw what he considered an 'ill acted' production at the Salisbury Court Theatre in 1661, and referred to it as 'a simple play' — 'simple', in this context, meaning 'foolish'. This would have been the first time the play was performed with women actors in the leading female roles, a practice that only began in this period. After two or three years in which there are records of further isolated performances, the play dropped out of the repertoire for 260 years.

Modern revivals

The French theatre prepared the ground for revivals of the play in England, with an adaptation by Maurice Maeterlinck, entitled simply *Annabella*, performed in Paris in 1894. Two private London performances, at the Shaftesbury Theatre by the Phoenix Company in 1923 and at the Arts Theatre Club in 1934, were well received, though the theme of incest and the visceral horror of the climax were played down in the first of these. Not until 1940 was the play restored to the public stage, in a production by the great actor-manager Donald Wolfit, who took the role of Giovanni, with Rosalind Iden as Annabella. The success of this production opened the way for subsequent revivals by a range of professional and amateur companies, until it was firmly re-established in the theatrical repertoire. However, it remains the only one of Ford's plays to have achieved fame and popularity in the modern theatre, perhaps because of the sensational nature of its subject (and title), which was particularly attractive to practitioners and audiences in the sexually-liberated and subversively-inclined 1960s.

In this period, the Lord Chamberlain's powers of theatre censorship were abolished, leading to revivals of Renaissance plays previously considered morally questionable, and to a greater frankness of stage presentation. In the 1977 Royal Shakespeare Company production of *'Tis Pity*, for example, Giovanni and Annabella's love-making had the naked actors simulating sexual intercourse, an effect whose shock value in a tiny studio theatre was matched by the terrifying proximity of the bloody climax.

As the shock value of incest has diminished slightly, directors of the play have sought various ways of redirecting the focus of attention in their productions. Some have emphasised the corrupt nature of the society by which the lovers are confined, while others have foregrounded the oppressive rituals of the Catholic Church, with its moral hypocrisy and spiritual bankruptcy highlighted by pervasive iconic imagery, from crucifixes and incense to confessionals and organ music. It is striking how many productions have given the play a modern setting, from the Actors' Company's *Dolce Vita*-style Italy of ice creams and Mafiosi in 1972, to the RSC's evocation of sober-suited ordinariness in 1991. The comic subplot has often been found embarrassing and unsatisfactory, and it was cut entirely from Giuseppe Patroni Griffi's 1973 film version.

Perhaps the most striking aspect of more recent performances has been the lack of success of actors in the leading roles, particularly that of Giovanni. Some of the best actors of their time have attempted the part, from Ian McKellen in 1972 to Rupert Graves in 1988 and Jude Law in 1999. Critics seem almost invariably to have found the role unsatisfactory in performance, with Giovanni emerging as an unsympathetic character, petulant and self-obsessed rather than tragically driven. Perhaps this simply reflects how the part is written.

The other principal difficulty for actors and directors lies in judging the appropriateness of audience laughter at the play's gory climax, where the image of Giovanni with Annabella's heart on his dagger frequently arouses titters and giggles rather than shock and horror. Critics who note such laughter in the theatre tend to distribute the blame fairly equally between the play, which is accused of veering into exaggerated melodrama instead of achieving tragic catharsis; the actors and director, who are held responsible for shortcomings in the staging and performance of the climactic scene; and the audience, whose laughter at violence and bloodshed supposedly reveals their emotional immaturity. Few directors have dared to assume that Ford actually demands laughter at this point, as part of that unsettling moral ambiguity espoused by many dramatists of the period. Instead, most directors attempt, with varying degrees of success, to suppress what is seen as a reaction that subverts the play's tragic impact.

Critical debate

The concept of Renaissance plays as objects of critical scrutiny did not really develop until the eighteenth century, and with the emergence of Shakespeare as the unassailable 'national poet', the work of his contemporaries and successors was inevitably relegated to subsidiary status. The plays of Marlowe, Jonson, Webster and Ford were judged against the 'genius' of Shakespeare and found wanting; in particular, the drama of the Caroline period was dismissed as 'decadent'. Ford and his contemporaries were accused of pandering to the tastes of an audience whose complacent sophistication could only be punctured by increasing sensationalism and prurience. Supposedly, the drama of the age was merely reflecting society's loss of moral direction, and the dramatic style of its writers was regarded as thin and enervated, in contrast to the linguistic richness and evocative imagery of Shakespeare.

However, Ford did find early critical supporters, from Charles Lamb in 1808 to Algernon Charles Swinburne in 1871, and complete editions of his plays were published in 1811 and 1827. In contrast, Francis Jeffrey and William Hazlitt were less appreciative of his qualities, and for many commentators the incestuous basis of its plot made 'Tis Pity virtually unperformable. The moral and sexual squeamishness of the nineteenth century led to the omission of the play from a collection of Ford's works in 1831, with the anonymous editor referring to it in his introduction as *Annabella and Giovanni*, a title he explained as a substitute 'for a much coarser one'. We may now laugh at such unenlightened attitudes but, as Martin Wiggins reports, even in the final years of the twentieth century, posters of student productions have been refused public display space, and in 1988 'the National Theatre found it impossible to obtain commercial sponsorship for [its] production without renaming the play — which, quite properly, it declined to do'.

The play's revival in the theatre coincided with a striking critical re-evaluation of Renaissance drama, with writers such as T. S. Eliot offering perceptive readings of play-wrights like Marlowe, Jonson, Middleton and Heywood. Eliot, though, is half-hearted in his praise of *'Tis Pity*, accusing the play of 'serious shortcomings', including the 'tedious' and 'superfluous' Hippolita subplot and the lack of 'general significance and emotional depth' that would justify its more sensational and violent elements.

Critical assessments of Renaissance drama may tell us more about the critics than the plays. Since the middle of the twentieth century, critical theory has developed into a bewildering web of competing orthodoxies in which not only the texts but students too may get left behind. While many A-level examiners still promote a kind of liberal humanist approach to literature, prioritising an informed personal response stemming from close textual scrutiny, the specifications now emphasise the contextualisation of texts, both in the cultural climate that produced them, and in the critical debate of succeeding ages.

However, modern critical approaches can still shed considerable light on the play. For example, **political criticism**, which might include **Marxist** analysis and **new historicism**, reminds us that literary texts are products of a particular set of sociopolitical circumstances from which they cannot be divorced, and that they are informed by a range of cultural preoccupations and anxieties that manifest themselves whether they are consciously intended by the writer or not. Crucial to *'Tis Pity She's a Whore*, for example, are issues such as the conflict between the Church's moral teachings and its involvement in worldly affairs; and contemporary attitudes to sex, love and marriage.

Feminist criticism, similarly, challenges assumptions about gender and exposes both the sexual stereotyping embodied in a text (''tis as common / To err in frailty as to be a woman', IV.3.144–45), and the way in which such stereotypes might be subverted. Whether a play like *'Tis Pity* exhibits feminist sympathies or merely accepts and endorses the patriarchal status quo and the misogyny of its time is an issue that can only enhance a consideration of the roles of Annabella, Hippolita, Putana and Philotis. Marion Lomax, in her essay on the play in the Introduction to her World's Classics edition (*'Tis Pity She's a Whore' and Other Plays*, Oxford University Press, 1995), gives a particularly astute feminist reading.

Other critical ideologies focus on language rather than social and historical context, and are based on complex matters of linguistic philosophy that can make them difficult for a non-specialist to grasp. **Structuralism** and **post-structuralism** see the relationship between language and meaning (or signifier and signified) as essentially fluid and shifting, revealing contradiction and ambiguity to such a degree that interpretation becomes no more than an identification of an ever-expanding range of possible meanings. In this context, as the critic Roland Barthes suggests, the role of the author is irrelevant, and any concept of authorial intention or control is a fallacy. This does not mean, however, that a text can mean anything we want it to.

The adherents of **deconstruction** are particularly adept at interrogating texts to find their contradictions and ambiguities, their generic discontinuities and their revealing gaps and silences. Deconstructionist critics often arrive at challenging and controversial interpretations that may sometimes seem perverse but have the merit of sending us back to the text to question it for ourselves. Examples of structuralist and deconstructionist criticism would include Susan Wiseman's analysis of the absence from the play of any real language for incest, and Lisa Hopkins's discussion of how language and meaning can be perverted by those who wield political or economic power.

Performance criticism looks at how the form of dramatic texts is determined by their basis in theatrical practice, examining them against what is known of the original stage conditions for which they were produced and the way they have been represented in other theatres and performance media. This approach questions the notion of a definitive text and undermines the concept of authorship, since theatre is essentially collaborative and ephemeral. In practice, most critical analysis, including your own, amounts to a fusion of different critical methods and ideologies.

The following quotations represent a range of critical approaches to Ford in general and *'Tis Pity She's a Whore* in particular:

> [The play] were to be commended, did not the author paint the incestuous love between Giovanni, and his sister Annabella, in too beautiful colours.
> (Gerard Langbaine, 1691)

> The catastrophe [i.e. climax] of [the play] is too shocking for an audience to bear.
> (David Erskine Baker, 1764)

> Nothing can be more revolting than the subject; and, therefore, the warmer and more glowing the pictures of love are worked up, the more reprehensible is the author.
> (Charles Dibdin, 1797)

> Ford was of the first order of Poets. He sought for sublimity, not by parcels in metaphors or visible images, but directly where she has her full residence in the heart of man, in the actions and sufferings of the greatest minds.
> (Charles Lamb, 1808)

> A play founded upon the incestuous and adulterous intercourse of a brother and sister, carries with it insuperable obstacles to its appearance upon a modern stage, nor could the beauty of its poetry have long supported, in any age, a representation so pregnant with horror.
> (William Gifford, 1811)

> Few [dramatists] have chosen a more unfortunate subject for the display of their talents.
> (Henry Weber, 1811)

> The repulsiveness of the story is what gives it its critical interest; for it is a studiously prosaic statement of facts, and naked declaration of passions.
> (William Hazlitt, 1819)

[Ford's plays] are merely exercises of style and effusions of wire-drawn sentiment. Where they have not the sting of illicit passion, they are quite pointless, and seem painted on gauze, or spun of cobwebs.

(William Hazlitt, 1819)

Giovanni comes upon the scene a professed and daring infidel, and [...] a shameless avower and justifier of his impure purpose: Annabella is not a jot behind him in precocity of vice.

(William Gifford, 1827)

[The play's poetry] flings a soft and soothing light over what in its natural state would glare with salutary and repulsive horror.

(William Gifford, 1827)

[Ford] delighted in the sensation of intellectual power, he found himself strong in the imagination of crime and agony; his moral sense was gratified by indignation at the dark possibilities of sin, by compassion for rare extremes of suffering. He abhorred vice — he admired virtue; but ordinary vice or modern virtue were, to him, as light wine to a dram drinker.

(Hartley Coleridge, 1840)

Nothing is more noticeable in this poet than the passionless reason and equable tone of style with which in his greatest works he treats of the deepest and most fiery passions.

(Algernon Charles Swinburne, 1871)

Of all the magnificent scenes which embody their terrible story the last is (as it should be) the most noble; it is indeed the finest scene in Ford.

(Algernon Charles Swinburne, 1871)

The tragic story is unrolled from first to last with fine truth and clear perceptions.

(Havelock Ellis, 1888)

[Ford] approaches the theme not with the temper of a stern realist bent on laying bare the secret links of cause and effect in a ferocious and ugly story of almost unmentionable lust and crime, but with the temper of a decadent romanticist bent on showing the enthralling power of physical beauty and the transfiguring power of passion.

(S. P. Sherman, 1915)

Giovanni is merely selfish and self-willed, of a temperament to want a thing the more because it is forbidden; Annabella is pliant, vacillating and negative: the one almost a monster of egotism, the other virtually a moral defective.

(T. S. Eliot, 1932)

The critics are in general agreement about one quality of [Ford's] writing, and that is the limited intensity of his emotional effects. Everything in Ford is focused to a single point; his plays live at the core, but they are not wholly alive.

(M. C. Bradbrook, 1935)

[In Renaissance tragedy] there is no simple faith in the man who rebels or in the law against which he rebels. There is a strong sense of sin, and of the arrogance that comes on a man as he hardens in sinning; there is a sense that he has had no choice; there is a sense that his fellows are not worthy of judging him. Above all, there is a strong sense of sympathy with the man who is apart from his fellows, making his challenge, facing his end.

(Clifford Leech, 1957)

Whatever criticisms may be made of the Friar, the impression still remains that Ford intended him as an admirable representative of orthodox morality.

(N. W. Bawcutt, 1966)

Society is shown as corrupt, and incestuous love as a relationship capable of deep and fragile beauty. (Brian Morris, 1968)

[The play's] modernity proves to be Ford's recognition [...] of a sterile, self-destructive world; one which he describes through the sexual relationship of the brother and sister as impotent and ineffective members of an incestuously structured and minded society. (Michael Scott, 1982)

By the constant comings and goings of his characters, Ford evokes a world of busy thoroughfares where the swordfight of Grimaldi and Vasques and the murder of Bergetto represent the all-too-familiar street violence typical of early modern London. (Verna Foster, 1988)

[There are many] indictments of the accuracy of language that we hear or have suggested to us in the play. [...] [W]e are shown that speech can be subjected to manipulation by those who possess either money or power, or both. The actions of the Cardinal reduce 'justice' to nothing but an empty word.

(Lisa Hopkins, 1994)

The proliferating subplots help to situate Giovanni and Annabella within a larger pattern of social relations and serve to modify any judgement on them. [...] It is obvious that Annabella's three suitors [...] throw Giovanni's many merits into sharp relief. (Rowland Wymer, 1995)

In 'Tis Pity women associated with dangerous sexual passions are controlled through the mutilation of their bodies. Here, Vasques burns Hippolita's body internally with the poison she intended for Soranzo; later he causes Putana's eyes to be put out and threatens to slit her nose, and the Cardinal finally has her burnt. Even Giovanni carves up his beloved sister to extract her heart. Only Philotis remains physically intact, and she survives by locking her body and her sexuality away in a convent.

(Marion Lomax, 1995)

Dramatists like Ford were largely preoccupied with questions of gender and sexuality which were of central concern to the audiences of their day. The history of the period […] is notable for the manner in which a variety of governmental and clerical institutions sought to regulate and police the sexuality of those subject to their scrutiny.   (Simon Barker, 1997)

Intensity of erotic passion, making every other kind of loyalty insignificant, imposes an obvious claim on audience sympathy. By making the love incestuous, Ford has, however, created a counter-current equally violent, equally uncompromising, and raised a conflict of total commitments […] between whole belief systems that no kindly friar can hope to bring to compromise.   (G. K. Hunter, 1997)

When Giovanni calls the concept of incest 'a customary form, from man to man' [I.1.25], he is reaching towards a truth. Incest is a social construction attached to a relatively unimportant biological fact.   (Derek Roper, 1997)

Figures such as Giovanni and Annabella suffer not because of their sins but because of their lower social position.   (Julie Sanders, 1999)

Useful quotations

Whether or not you are allowed to have your text with you in an exam, it is useful to have learned a range of quotations covering various aspects of the play. The best quotations to learn are those that could be used to illustrate more than one area.

Consider the usefulness of the quotations selected below in terms of what they might show about character, themes, language, imagery or dramatic effect.

Act I scene 1

Must I not do what all men else may — love?
(Giovanni equivocates about his relationship with his sister)

                 Hast thou left the schools
Of knowledge, to converse with lust and death?
For death waits on thy lust.
(The Friar bemoans Giovanni's moral deterioration)

Act I scene 2

I would not for my wealth my daughter's love
Should cause the spilling of one drop of blood.
(Florio is horrified at the violent dispute between his daughter's suitors)

... see; what blessed shape
Of some celestial creature now appears?
(Annabella expresses her worship of Giovanni)

'Tis not, I know,
My lust, but 'tis my fate that leads me on.
(Giovanni shifts the responsibility for his feelings from himself to destiny)

Rip up my bosom: there thou shalt behold
A heart in which is writ the truth I speak.
(Giovanni chillingly anticipates, in mirror-image, the play's ending)

I have asked counsel of the holy Church,
Who tells me I may love you.
(Giovanni misleads Annabella with a blatant lie)

Act I scene 3

I would not have her marry wealth, but love.
(Florio seems like a reasonable father)

Act II scene 1

...if a young wench feel the fit upon her, let her take anybody, father or brother, all is one.
(Putana justifies incest and prioritises sexual pleasure)

Act II scene 2

'Tis not your new mistress,
Your goodly Madam Merchant, shall triumph
On my dejection.
(Hippolita shows contempt for Annabella's social class)

Revenge shall sweeten what my griefs have tasted.
(Hippolita finds solace in thoughts of revenge)

Act II scene 3

Alas, I fear
You mean some strange revenge.
(Philotis perceptively notes her uncle's motives)

Act II scene 4

I will marry you in spite of your teeth.
(Bergetto's letter, read by Poggio, reveals his romantic inclinations. N.B. He is not literally disparaging the state of Annabella's teeth; the phrase simply means 'whether you like it or not')

Act II scene 5

Peace! Thou hast told a tale whose every word
Threatens eternal slaughter to the soul.
(The Friar's horror increases…)

O ignorance in knowledge!
(…and he condemns Giovanni's intellectual sophistry)

Act II scene 6

That's a blessèd man,
A man made up of holiness.
(Florio praises the Friar — but how justifiably?)

By this light, she had a face methinks worth twenty of you, Mistress Annabella.
(Bergetto knows how to flatter a girl)

Act III scene 1

Does my uncle think to make me a baby still?
(Bergetto resents his uncle's treatment of him)

Act III scene 2

SORANZO: Did you but see my heart, then would you swear —
ANNABELLA: That you were dead.
(Annabella punctures Soranzo's romantic eloquence, and again foreshadows the end of the play)

Not hope of what you have, but what you are
Have drawn me on.
(Soranzo disclaims financial considerations in wooing Annabella)

Act III scene 3

O me,
I have a world of business in my head!
(Giovanni's mental resources are overtaxed by Annabella's pregnancy)

Act III scene 4

Welcome, religious friar, you are one
That still bring blessing to the place you come to.
(Florio still believes in the Friar's virtues)

Act III scene 5

So, if this hit, I'll laugh and hug revenge.
(Richardetto relishes the prospect of vengeance)

Act III scene 6

...there lies the wanton
On racks of burning steel, whiles in his soul
He feels the torment of his raging lust.
(The Friar paints a vivid picture of the eternal torment that Annabella is risking...)

But soft, methinks I see repentance work
New motions in your heart.
(...and his words seem to have achieved the desired effect)

Act III scene 7

O my master, my master, my master!
(Poggio is distraught at Bergetto's death)

Act III scene 8

I am infinitely yours.
(Vasques manipulates Hippolita with machiavellian policy)

Act III scene 9

The Cardinal is noble: he no doubt
Will give true justice.
(Richardetto is sadly deluded...)

Come, come, Donado, there's no help in this
When cardinals think murder's not amiss.
Great men may do their wills, we must obey,
But Heaven will judge them for't another day.
(...and Florio responds to political corruption with simple faith in divine justice)

Act IV scene 1

Foolish woman, thou art now like a firebrand, that hath kindled others and
burnt thyself.
(Vasques revels in Hippolita's self-destruction)

I fear the event: that marriage seldom's good,
Where the bride-banquet so begins in blood.
(The Friar states the rather obvious)

Act IV scene 2

        …there is one
Above begins to work.
(Richardetto sees the workings of divine justice begin to stir…)

All human worldly courses are uneven:
No life is blessèd but the way to heaven.
(…and urges the religious life on Philotis)

Act IV scene 3

Come, strumpet, famous whore!
(Soranzo anticipates the Cardinal's moral judgement on Annabella)

        …'twas not for love
I chose you, but for honour.
(Annabella comes clean with her husband)

Not know it, strumpet! I'll rip up thy heart
And find it there.
(Soranzo unknowingly anticipates Annabella's fate)

Sir, in any case smother your revenge: leave the scenting-out your wrongs to
me.
(Vasques counsels policy rather than open vengeance)

My reason tells me now that 'tis as common
To err in frailty as to be a woman.
(Soranzo expresses conventional contempt for women)

I carry hell about me: all my blood
Is fired in swift revenge.
(Soranzo is ill at ease)

Act V scene 1

A wretched, woeful woman's tragedy.
(Annabella assesses her situation in terms of dramatic genre)

Act V scene 2

Revenge is all the ambition I aspire;
To that I'll climb or fall. My blood's on fire!
(Soranzo's need for vengeance overwhelms him)

Act V scene 3

Busy opinion is an idle fool.
(Giovanni belittles conventional morality...)

The hell you oft have prompted is nought else
But slavish and fond superstitious fear.
(...and attacks core religious beliefs)

I must not stay
To know thy fall: back to Bologna I
With speed will haste, and shun this coming blow.
(The Friar abdicates his responsibilities)

Act V scene 4

What you do
Is noble and an act of brave revenge.
(Soranzo persuades the banditti of their moral justification in being instruments of his revenge — as if they cared!)

Act V scene 5

...know that now there's but a dining-time
'Twixt us and our confusion. Let's not waste
These precious hours in vain and useless speech.
(Annabella attempts to impart a sense of urgency to Giovanni)

ANNABELLA: What mean's this?
GIOVANNI: To save thy fame, and kill thee in a kiss.
Thus die, and die by me, and by my hand.
Revenge is mine; honour doth love command.
(Giovanni rationalises his killing of Annabella)

Act V scene 6

> 'Tis a heart,
> A heart, my lords, in which is mine entombed.
> *(Giovanni finally has possession of Annabella's heart)*

> I rejoice that a Spaniard outwent an Italian in revenge.
> *(Vasques enjoys a moment of national pride)*

> Of one so young, so rich in Nature's store,
> Who could not say, 'Tis pity she's a whore?
> *(The Cardinal makes his judgement)*

Selected glossary of literary terms

Note: terms are defined here in their literary sense; they often have alternative meanings in other contexts. Cross-references to other glossary entries are printed in bold.

allegory   a literary form in which the characters and events in the story represent something in a **symbolic** way and offer a moral lesson. Allegories often feature characters who are **personified** abstractions.

alliteration   the repetition of initial consonant sounds in words placed comparatively near to each other. This can be emphatic or can enhance the effect of **onomatopoeia**, e.g. 'Burn, blood, and boil in vengeance!' (IV.1.93).

allusion   a passing reference to something — an event, person, myth, literary work, piece of music — which the writer does not explain, presumably expecting it to be within the reader's general knowledge.

ambiguous   having two or more possible interpretations, but leaving in doubt which is correct. Textual ambiguity may be deliberate or accidental.

ambivalent   having contradictory feelings or attitudes towards something; having either or both of two contrary or parallel values, qualities or meanings.

antithesis   a balancing of words or phrases of opposite meaning, e.g. 'in such games as those they *lose* that *win*' (I.1.63).

archaic   words and expressions no longer in everyday use; old-fashioned.

aside	a remark spoken by a character in a play that is unheard by some or all of the other characters on stage. It may be shared directly with the audience.
assonance	identical vowel sounds in words placed comparatively near to each other in a piece of writing to create particular effects of emphasis, echo, **onomatopoeia** etc., e.g. 'choked with smoky fogs' (III.6.12).
atmosphere	the emotional **tone** conjured up by a particular use of language; the mood or feeling created.
bathos	an anticlimax, in which there is a fall 'from the sublime to the ridiculous'.
blank verse	unrhymed **iambic pentameter**.
blazon	a form of love poetry cataloguing a woman's qualities in a metaphorical sequence.
caesura	a mid-line break in a **verse** line, coinciding with the end of a grammatical unit, e.g. 'Your grace's pardon: thus long I lived disguised' (V.6.151).
caricature	an exaggerated, unrealistic character in fiction or drama, built around a limited number of character traits such as greed or naïvety.
characterisation	the techniques by which a writer creates fictional or dramatic characters. These might include description, **dialogue**, **symbolism**, authorial comment, interior monologue, **soliloquy** etc.
climax	a moment of intensity and power to which a play or story has been leading.
colloquial	the language of speech rather than writing, informal in grammar and vocabulary, possibly using dialect or employing the phraseology of slang.
comedy	a dramatic **genre** in which events reach a positive outcome, often concluding in betrothal or marriage, or in the exposure of vice and folly. Although comedy often contains elements of humour, this is not a prerequisite of the genre.
denouement	the unfolding of the final stages of a dramatic or fictional **plot**, usually at or just after the **climax**.
dialogue	the direct speech of characters in fiction or drama engaged in conversation.
diction	a writer's choice of words. Diction may be formal, **colloquial**, poetic, **ironic**, artificial etc. It helps to create the **tone** and mood of a piece of writing, and in drama can be an instrument of **characterisation**.

dramatic	pertaining to the **genre** of drama. If you are asked to consider whether part of a play is 'dramatic', you are not being asked to say whether it is *exciting*, but whether it contributes to the overall impact of the play.
dramatic irony	a discrepancy between the perceptions of the audience and those of the characters in a play. Dramatic irony may create humour or tension.
eclectic	drawing on a wide range of reference from diverse sources.
emotive language	language that arouses an emotional response in the reader or hearer.
end-stopped line	a line of **verse** in which the grammatical sense is completed at the end of the line, e.g. 'The hope of me will hinder such a hope' (II.6.50).
enjamb(e)ment	running the sense from one line of **verse** over to the next without a pause at the end of the line, e.g. 'My tortured soul / Hath felt affliction in the heat of death' (I.2.208–09).
epilogue	a speech that rounds off a play, either summing up its events, reflecting on its conclusion or inviting the audience's applause. It may be spoken by a character, an actor stepping out of character or a chorus figure.
exposition	the delivery of crucial information to the audience, usually at the start of a play, filling in the background to the characters and the **plot**.
feminine ending	a light or unstressed syllable at the end of a line of **verse**, e.g. 'And hear you, daughter, see you use him nobly' (III.2.7).
genre	a classification of literary texts (or other artistic forms) according to type. *'Tis Pity She's a Whore* might be classified as **tragedy** or, more specifically, **revenge tragedy**. Genre classification can be unhelpful in simplifying complex works into convenient terminology. *'Tis Pity She's a Whore*, for example, also contains comic elements.
hyperbole	exaggeration, usually for poetic or **dramatic** effect.
iambic pentameter	a line of **verse** consisting of five iambic feet (see **metrical foot**).
imagery	a pattern of related images that helps to build up mood and **atmosphere**, deepen our response to characters or develop the **themes** of a literary work.
incongruity	when something is or seems out of place in its context, for example a joke at the **climax** of a **tragedy**.

irony	a discrepancy between the actual and implied meaning of language, illustrated in its crudest verbal form by sarcasm. Irony can be complex and subtle in the hands of great writers, though it can be difficult to pick up the ironic **tone**. See also **dramatic irony**.
machiavel	a devious, scheming politician, based on an English misreading of the works of the Italian political philosopher Niccolò Machiavelli; a common **stereotype** of Renaissance drama, best represented in *'Tis Pity She's a Whore* by Vasques.
malcontent	someone with a grudge against society, who adopts an air of bitterness and melancholy; a common **stereotype** of Renaissance drama, partly illustrated in *'Tis Pity* in the character of Vasques.
masque	a form of entertainment combining elaborate poetry, music and scenic spectacle, particularly popular at the courts of James I and Charles I. Dramatists of the period often introduced masque-like elements into their plays, such as Hippolita's masque for Soranzo and Annabella's wedding.
melodramatic	exaggeratedly dramatic and sensational, appealing crudely to the emotions.
metaphor	an imaginative identification between one thing and another, e.g. Soranzo's reference to Annabella as 'this most precious jewel' (IV.1.10).
metatheatrical	a self-conscious awareness in a play of its status as a theatrical performance. Such an awareness might work through the persistent use of theatrical **metaphor**, or through more substantial devices such as a play within the play.
metre	a particular pattern of rhythmical organisation based on the number and distribution of stressed syllables in a line. There are a number of common metres in English verse, the most common being **iambic pentameter**.
metrical foot	one unit of a line of **verse**, consisting of two or three syllables with different patterns of **stress**. For example, an **iambic** foot has two syllables, the second of which is stressed. The **metre** is determined by the number of particular kinds of feet in a line.
morality play	religious drama popular in fifteenth- and sixteenth-century England, often in the form of **allegory**, peopled by **personified** abstractions such as Knowledge, and representative characters like Everyman.

onomatopoeia	the use of words that imitate the sounds they describe (e.g. fizz, spit, crash); or a combination of words where the sound seems to echo the sense. **Assonance** and **alliteration** can often be used to create an onomatopoeic effect.
oxymoron	a condensed **antithesis**; usually a phrase of two words, apparently opposite in meaning, which ought to cancel each other out, e.g. 'darkness visible' (John Milton, *Paradise Lost*); 'oppressive liberty' (George Eliot, *Middlemarch*); 'delicious bane' (*'Tis Pity*, II.2.160)
personification	a variety of **metaphor** which attributes human qualities to something inanimate or abstract, e.g. 'The hand of goodness / Hath been a shield for me against my death' (IV.1.7–8).
plagiarism	stealing someone else's ideas and passing them off as your own; intellectual theft. Writers are often accused of this, but it was not regarded as particularly serious in Ford's time, when playwrights frequently plundered the work of other writers for ideas.
plot	the organisation and structuring of the narrative and its characters in a novel or play.
prologue	a speech that precedes the main action of a play.
promptbook	the annotated copy of a playscript used in managing and running a theatrical performance.
prose	the language of everyday speech and writing, distinguished from poetry or **verse**.
pun	a play on words, often for humorous effect. When Putana suggests that soldiers often have 'some privy maim or other that mars their standing upright' (I.2.79–80), she is playing on the dual associations of 'privy', meaning hidden, but suggesting the private parts; and also using 'standing upright' in the lewd sense of having an erection, as well as its literal meaning.
quarto	small-format early printed book, usually containing the equivalent of a single play.
resolution	the tying up of loose ends at the end of a fictional or dramatic narrative, during or immediately after the **denouement**.
revenge tragedy	a popular **dramatic genre** of the late sixteenth and early seventeenth century, with central characters motivated by vengeance, against individuals or society in general.

rhetoric	the art of using language to persuade. Rhetoric was taught as a subject in Renaissance schools, modelled on classical examples, identifying a range of specific linguistic techniques which a good persuasive speaker or writer was expected to use.
rhyme	identical sounds repeated at the ends of **verse** lines in a variety of patterns. The last stressed vowel sound and everything that follows it should be identical, e.g. yet/met, store/whore (V.6.156–59)
rhyming couplet	a pair of adjacent rhyming lines.
satire	a literary form in which people, institutions and aspects of human behaviour are attacked through humour, by being made to appear ridiculous.
simile	an imaginative comparison of one thing with another, drawing attention to itself by using the words 'like' or 'as', e.g. 'the breath that vents it /Will, like a bubble, break itself at last' (IV.1.44–45).
soliloquy	a speech in a play, usually of some length, delivered by a character alone on stage. Characters may address the audience directly, or we may feel we are sharing their thoughts. Traditionally, soliloquies were considered to reveal the genuine feelings of a character, free of equivocation and deception.
sonnet	a poem of 14 lines, in iambic pentameter, with a regular rhyming pattern; traditionally, but not exclusively, about love.
sources	the inspirations, drawn from history, mythology or other literary and dramatic works, that writers build into their own artistic vision.
stereotype	a fictional or **dramatic** character conforming to a narrow set of characteristics assumed to be typical of a particular group.
stress	the natural emphasis we put on particular syllables in words when we speak. Used to construct rhythmical patterns of **metre** when composing **verse**.
subplot	a subordinate storyline in a fictional or **dramatic** narrative, with its own set of characters, that works alongside or interlocks with the main **plot**.
subtext	the meaning implied by or underlying the explicit language of a text.

symbolism	the explicit or implied representation of a thing or idea by something else. A dove may symbolise peace, or a river life. Literary and **dramatic** symbolism may be complex, for example the culminating symbol of Annabella's heart.
tableau	the visual arrangement of characters and objects as if in a picture.
theme	an issue or idea developed in a work of literature. Most complex texts have a variety of themes.
tone	a particular quality in the use of language that may indicate the writer's or speaker's attitude to the reader or listener, or may create a particular mood or **atmosphere**. A tone may be formal, sincere, pompous, gloomy, ironic, solemn, cheerful etc.
tragedy	a **dramatic genre** focusing on the downfall or death of one or two central characters, usually of elevated social status.
unities	'rules' of drama, originally propounded by Aristotle in the fourth century BC, that the action of a play should consist of one unified **plot**, enacted in one location and taking place within a single day. Like most English dramatists of his time, Ford ignores the unities in *'Tis Pity*.
verse	language organised according to its rhythmical qualities into regular patterns of **metre**. Verse may or may not **rhyme**, but is usually set out in lines.

Questions & Answers

LITERATURE

Essay questions, specimen plans and notes

Coursework essays

In choosing a coursework essay, you must always check with your teacher that it fits the requirements of the course you are following. For example, it would be foolish to choose a title that focuses on Assessment Objectives that are not covered in the coursework part of your specification.

You may have valid ideas of your own for an essay title or subject. Again, these should be discussed with your teacher. Make sure you know the number of words allowed for the essay.

Suggested titles

1 **What kind of a play is *'Tis Pity She's a Whore?* How successfully do you think it works as a text for the theatre?**
   Here are some ideas for tackling this essay:
   - discussion of revenge tragedy in the context of Jacobean and Caroline theatre
   - deliberate parallels with *Romeo and Juliet*
   - staging requirements of indoor theatre for which it was written
   - exploiting contemporary taste for sensational and controversial subject matter
   - analysis of structure of play, including function of subplots, balance of serious and comic, use of masque
   - the play's portrayal of its society, and the effect of setting it in Italy
   - effectiveness of the play's characterisation and the scope for actors to create an impact, both individually and in relationships with others
   - examination of some key scenes and their effectiveness
   - the play's language and its variety – verse and prose, colloquial, poetic, melodramatic
   - effect on the audience, e.g. how moving, tragic impact, comic elements, the issue of laughter at the climax

2 **How is the world of the play created through language and action? What kinds of stage setting, costume and lighting might enhance the play's impact in a production?**
3 **What is your response to the characters of Giovanni and Annabella? Do you find them attractive and sympathetic, and are they worthy of tragic status?**
4 **Explore the character and role of any one of the principal characters in the play.**
5 **Choose two characters who offer interesting points for comparison and contrast. Write an essay comparing their characters and roles in the play, saying what you**

thought of them, and assessing how effectively Ford portrays them. (Suggestions: Bonaventura and the Cardinal; Bonaventura and Putana; Annabella and Hippolita; Soranzo and Bergetto; Vasques and Poggio; Philotis and Putana; Florio and Donado.)

6 How does Ford present the women in the play? Examine the characterisation and roles of the female characters.

7 Write about the different kinds of humour and comic effect in the play. How do you respond to the humour in the context of a tragedy? Do you think Ford is always in control of the points at which an audience might laugh?

8 Write about some of the themes you consider to be important in the play and show how they are developed.

9 Write about the imagery of the play and the effects it creates.

10 Choose one scene, or a self-contained section within a scene, and give a full analysis of it, commenting on what it reveals of characters and themes; its dramatic effect; its supporting imagery; and anything else that interests you.

11 Choose one scene and describe how you would present it on stage. (You will need to give some preliminary account of the type of theatre you envisage as well as the overall production style.)

12 Imagine you are a director who wishes to stage a production of *'Tis Pity She's a Whore*. Explain in a preliminary note what kind of theatre or company you work for (large or small; professional or amateur; rich or poor; commercial or subsidised; indoor or open-air; traditional or experimental; touring or home-based). Then write a letter to your artistic director or board explaining your reasons for considering this a good play to stage and giving an outline of your approach to the production.

13 Write a letter to an actor preparing to play the role of *either* Giovanni *or* Annabella, explaining how you think they should approach the part and giving guidance on their performance in particular scenes.

14 How useful have you found it to study the play in the context of Ford and his time?

15 How has your understanding of the play been enhanced by your reading of a variety of literary criticism? What critical views have you encountered that you consider particularly interesting, revealing or controversial?

16 Write a comparison of *'Tis Pity She's a Whore*, or any appropriate aspect of it, with another Elizabethan, Jacobean or Caroline play that you know well. (*Romeo and Juliet*, *Women Beware Women* or *The Broken Heart* would be good choices.)

17 Write a review of any production of the play — on stage, film or television. You should comment on the interpretation of the play and the characters; the sets, costumes, music, lighting, performances; and anything else you consider important. If you have seen more than one production, you could write a comparison.

Tackling production-related questions

There can be no substitute for seeing a play in performance — preferably on stage. There is an electricity about live performance, a sense of danger and risk as well as of shared experience, that cannot be captured on film or television. Your response to a production will be as personal and subjective as that to any other cultural experience. You should, however, make some attempt to understand what it is trying to achieve, and judge it accordingly.

'Tis Pity She's a Whore is a brilliant performance piece, but you should be prepared for disappointments. Giovanni is a difficult role for an actor to bring off successfully; the comic subplot is hard to animate effectively for a modern audience; and the notoriously challenging final scene can often arouse unwanted laughter if it is not carefully handled.

The impact of a production may depend on the kind of theatre in which it is staged. A small, intimate theatre, with the audience on three or four sides, can offer a kind of psychologically intense and detailed performance that may be more difficult to achieve in a large theatre with a proscenium stage. A large theatre, though, has more scope for spectacular presentation.

Clues to a production's approach and emphasis can often be found in publicity materials such as brochures and posters, and in the programme. These are always worth a look, both before and after you have seen the show.

- What signals do they give about the play itself and the approach taken to it in the production?

Theatres today rarely have stage curtains that are closed before the performance.

- What clues were there to the production style in what you saw as you took your place in the theatre before the play started?

The opening moments of a production signal its style, too. Directors will not necessarily begin *'Tis Pity* with Giovanni and the Friar in conversation. Perhaps there will be a church ceremony at the start; or a brief evocation of Parma's social world; or some action representing Florio's dinner party, to create the atmosphere before the dialogue begins.

- How did the production begin? Was there music, a visual display or dumb show, the swift creation of a stage setting, or anything else not specified in the text?
- What was the intention behind such an opening, and how effective was it?

When reflecting on a production, there are various aspects to consider. These are discussed below.

The world of the play

- What was the overall setting of the play? Was it performed in the period in which the story is set, the period in which the play was written, in a modern setting, or some other period? Perhaps there was a more eclectic approach, with elements from a variety of periods and cultures?

- Why do you think this decision had been made? Did it work? In particular, if a modern setting was chosen, did you find it helped you to understand the social and political aspects of the play, or was it jarring to see the characters using guns, mobile phones and laptops while speaking of daggers, letters and classical mythology?
- How was the play's world represented visually? Was much scenery or furniture used? Did this change between scenes? Was there any use of backdrops or projections? What kind of colour schemes were employed? How were lighting, music and sound effects used to enhance the mood and atmosphere of the settings?
- How were the characters costumed? Did their costumes suggest appropriate ideas about their personality, social status and dramatic role? What costume changes did characters have?
- Were there any particularly striking effects? How were key moments staged — the fight between Vasques and Grimaldi, Hippolita's masque, Soranzo dragging Annabella by her hair, Giovanni's entry with her heart on his dagger?

The use of the text

- Were you aware of any cuts, alterations, additions or transpositions? Why do you think such textual changes were made?
- Were any characters doubled? Was this merely due to expediency, or did it make a particular point?
- Where did any intervals come in the play? Were they at appropriate moments, or did they break the dramatic continuity?
- Was the text spoken well? Was the story told clearly? Was any special emphasis given to particular words, lines or speeches?
- Was the performance paced effectively?

The performances

In responding to actors' performances, it is particularly important to recognise the difference between a bad performance and a performance that differs from your own understanding of a role. A bad performance might be technically inadequate — inaudible, lacking in energy and charisma, delivering lines without apparently understanding their meaning etc. An interpretation of a role may be misguided or perverse but performed brilliantly, and should cause you to reassess your own interpretation.

- Which performances were most powerful and effective? What made them so?
- Were you surprised by any of the actors' interpretations?
- Did any roles come to life in performance in a way that they didn't when you were studying the text?
- Did the actors work well together as an ensemble?

Your overall response

- Did the production work well for you as a theatrical entertainment? Were you engrossed, amused, excited, moved or bored? How can you explain these responses?
- Did the production do justice to the play? Did it change your view of the play?

Theatre is a collaborative activity, and in writing about a production you need to show some awareness of the roles of the various practitioners. Those in the front line are obviously the actors, but their performances will have been shaped by the director, who is also responsible for the overall concept and interpretation. Much of what you remember from a production, though, may well be the contribution of the designer, while the practicalities of the smooth running of each performance are the responsibility of the stage manager. Other roles, such as those of lighting designer, sound designer, composer and music director, speak for themselves.

Exam essays

You can use the questions below as the basis of your own exam practice: to refine your brainstorming and planning skills, or to tackle a complete essay in the appropriate time limit. Choose the type of question that is relevant for the specification you are following: in AQA (A), for example, the questions normally focus on the play's original cultural context and the way subsequent cultural changes have affected its interpretation. Remember to refer to the *play* and the *audience*, not the *book* and the *reader*. Remain imaginatively aware of the play's *performance* potential.

Whole text questions

Questions 15, 16, 19, 20, 21, 23, 31, 32, 33, 34, 35, 36, 38, 39, 40, 45 are more suitable for open book exams.

Genre and context

1 How useful is it to consider *'Tis Pity She's a Whore* as a revenge tragedy?
2 How might the play's original audiences have responded to its portrayal of the Catholic Church through the characters of the Friar and the Cardinal?
3 Do you think the play reflects in any way the political situation at the time it was written, particularly the increasing tensions between King Charles I and his parliament?
4 How are Renaissance attitudes to women reflected in the play? Do you think Ford presents the female characters sympathetically?
5 What is your understanding of tragedy, and how far do you think *'Tis Pity She's a Whore* conforms to traditional expectations of tragic drama?

6 How differently do you think modern audiences would respond to the play, compared with audiences of Ford's time? Which particular aspects of the play might arouse the most divergent reactions?

Characters

7 Martin Wiggins comments that, in performance, Giovanni 'is a role which consistently seems to disappoint'. Why do you think this might be?

8 How do you respond to the view that Annabella is a much less sympathetic character than Giovanni?

9 Compare and contrast the characters of Soranzo and Bergetto.

10 Examine Ford's portrayal of Bonaventura and Putana, focusing on their roles as mentors to Giovanni and Annabella.

11 Do you agree that Hippolita is portrayed melodramatically?

12 How effectively does Ford present the character of Vasques?

13 What is the function of Richardetto and Philotis in the play?

14 Some productions of the play have removed the role of Bergetto. What would the play gain and/or lose without him?

15 Choose any scene in which *either* Giovanni and Annabella *or* Annabella and Soranzo interact powerfully. How does Ford present the relationship between them in your chosen scene?

16 Write about the dramatic impact of *one* of the encounters between Giovanni and Bonaventura in the play.

17 How dramatically does Ford present Florio and Donado in the play?

18 Assess the role of the Cardinal in the play as a whole.

Setting and atmosphere

19 According to Verna Foster, Ford 'evokes a world of busy thoroughfares' where the street violence and the murder of Bergetto are 'typical of early modern London'. How does Ford create this atmosphere in any *two* scenes of the play?

20 How does Ford evoke a combination of celebration and horror in the play's two onstage feasting scenes (IV.1 and V.6)?

21 Examine Ford's use of religious imagery, particularly in III.6, to create a sense of ominous foreboding.

22 What impression does Ford give of social class divisions in the world of the play?

23 How would you create the atmosphere of any *one* scene of the play in a modern stage production? Consider the use of set, costumes, lighting, music, movement and sound effects, and explain how these would support specific features of the text.

Themes

24 How would you respond to the view that incest is not the *theme* of the play, but merely its *subject*?

25 How broad is the play's attack on religious hypocrisy — or do you think it simply reflects the anti-Catholic prejudice of its time?

26 How far does Ford engage explicitly with the issue of women's status in society?

27 Examine the variety of relationships in the play that demonstrate the extremes of love and lust. Is there shown to be a clear division between the two qualities?

28 What does the play have to say about the qualities of justice and mercy?

29 Soranzo and Giovanni both talk about 'brave revenge', and justify their actions as a requirement of 'honour'. Do you think the play shares their view of honour and revenge?

30 Characters in the play persistently deceive others through lying, disguise and false appearances. What overall view does the play seem to take of this issue?

Structure and dramatic effect

31 Write an analysis of the play's five-act structure.

32 Explain how the play is partly structured around disrupted feasting.

33 How does Ford move between serious and comic scenes in the early part of the play, and how effective is this contrast of mood?

34 What is there in the final scene of the play (V.6) that might arouse laughter, and do you consider such a response to be appropriate?

35 How well are the subplots involving *either* Bergetto *or* Hippolita integrated into the play's overall structure?

36 Choose *one* scene of the play that you consider represents an effective dramatic climax, and examine how Ford achieves this effect.

Language

37 What are some of the recurring images that Ford uses in the play, and what effect does such imagery have?

38 Track the recurring image of the heart throughout the play and attempt to assess its symbolic significance.

39 Examine two or three of the prose sections in the play. Consider aspects of Ford's prose style, suggest why these sections are in prose not verse, and assess their impact in the dramatic context.

40 How do you respond to the commonly held critical view that Ford's style is flat and colourless? Use close textual analysis to support your argument.

Shifting attitudes to the play resulting from cultural changes

41 Early critics of the play could hardly get beyond its abhorrent portrayal of incest. What might we find of greater interest in the play, now that incest is less shocking to us?

42 Ford and his fellow dramatists of the 1620s and 1630s were long regarded as decadent and sensational, revealing a huge falling off from the plays of

Shakespeare. Why do you think more recent critics have reassessed the quality of plays such as *'Tis Pity She's a Whore*?

43 In 1966, N. W. Bawcutt considered that Ford intended the Friar to be 'an admirable representative of orthodox morality'. Do you think audiences in Ford's time would have agreed? How do *you* view the Friar now?

44 How might our response to Ford's portrayal of women be different from that of readers and audiences of over 100 years ago?

45 When Shakespeare was considered the greatest English dramatist, his richly metaphorical, poetic style was regarded as the model for verse drama, with dramatists like Ford falling far short of his qualities. Present-day critics have been much more positive in their analysis of Ford's style. What qualities in Ford's writing do you think might now be especially valued?

Passage-based questions

When tackling passage-based analysis, depending on the precise nature of the question, you should consider the points outlined below:

- Is the section in prose, verse or a mixture of the two? What is notable about the way these language modes are used?
- What is its place in the development of the plot?
- What is going on between the characters present, and what is the impact of any entrances and exits?
- What is the impact of characters who say little in the section?
- How does the language of the scene reveal character?
- What is the balance between dialogue and soliloquy, longer and shorter speeches?
- How does the section support the wider imagery and themes of the play?
- How is the stage picture, together with action and movement, suggested through the dialogue and any stage directions?
- Are there any levels of irony or dramatic irony in the sequence?
- Which characters engage the audience's sympathy, and why?
- What is the function of the set section in the dramatic structure of the play? Are there any parallels or contrasts with other episodes? What would the play lose without this section?

1 Reread the opening scene of the play between Giovanni and Bonaventura. How does Ford establish their characters in this scene?

2 Look again at the opening of Act I scene 2, as far as Annabella's line, 'Would you would leave me' (line 69). How does Ford use language, verse and prose, physical action and the stage space to create social context, character and relationships, plot and situation?

3 Study Giovanni's soliloquy at I.2.140–58, and Soranzo's at II.2.1–18. Write a comparison of the two speeches, showing how Ford creates the contrast between their characters.

4   Examine Giovanni's dialogue with Annabella from I.2.159–262 and compare it with their subsequent encounter at II.1.1–34. How does Ford portray their developing relationship in these two scenes?

5   How does Ford establish Bergetto's character and his relationship with Poggio in their first two appearances, I.2.100–17 and I.3.29–85?

6   Examine how Ford introduces Hippolita into the play in Act I scene 2 and consider how the audience might respond to her.

7   Write an analysis of Act II scene 5, commenting on how Giovanni's relationship with the Friar has changed since Act I scene 1.

8   How does Ford create both humour and suspense in Act II scene 6?

9   Examine the interview between Annabella and Soranzo, observed by Giovanni, at III.2.15–72. Analyse the different ways in which Annabella uses language to avoid committing herself to responding positively to Soranzo's wooing, and assess the dramatic impact of the scene.

10 Reread Act III scene 7, the scene of Bergetto's death. Write a close analysis of the scene, focusing on its dramatic impact and assessing the extent to which it is, or should be, comic.

11 Assuming that a modern production of the play would require *one* interval, argue for the advantages and disadvantages of placing it after Act III scene 9 and after Act IV scene 1.

12 Look again at Act IV scene 1 and consider its dramatic effect, both in terms of the stage spectacle and the spoken text. Do not concentrate exclusively on Hippolita, Soranzo and Vasques, but give some attention also to the characters who speak least in the scene and suggest how the actors might react.

13 Reread Act IV scene 3, as far as Vasques's entry at line 76. How does Ford make this encounter between Soranzo and Annabella gripping and shocking?

14 Look again at the second part of Act IV scene 3, from Vasques's entrance at line 76 to the end of the scene. How does Ford present Vasques in this sequence?

15 Study Act V scene 3. How do you respond to Giovanni in this scene?

16 Reread Act V scene 5. How far do you consider this scene to be a fitting conclusion to the relationship of Annabella and Giovanni? How does Ford manipulate tension and direct our sympathies in this scene?

17 What are some of the challenges posed to actors, directors and audiences in Act V scene 6? How effectively do you think that this scene concludes the play?

Essay plans

1   *'Tis Pity She's a Whore* remained unperformed on the English stage from the early 1660s until 1923. Subsequently, it has become one of the most frequently staged plays of Shakespeare's contemporaries. What do you think accounts for both its neglect and its revival of popularity?

Possible ideas to include in a plan

Introduction

- evidence of popularity of play in its own time
- subsequent attitudes to play determined largely by cultural changes

Reasons for neglect, 1660–1923

- largely occasioned by sensational nature of its theme – incest aroused feelings of abhorrence, and William Gifford (1811) considered this made it unstageable
- equally, the shockingly violent conclusion – Annabella's skewered heart – would have been considered outrageous
- in addition, the Romantic period increasingly venerated Shakespeare, and his contemporaries were consigned to subsidiary status; in particular, late Jacobean and Caroline playwrights were accused of decadence (sensationalism for its own sake) and their language was seen to fall short of Shakespeare's high standards; give examples

Revivals in early twentieth century

- the rise of modernism also involved a reassessment of the past; modernist writers like T. S. Eliot began reassessing early modern drama
- various theatre practitioners became interested in early theatre practice as a reaction against the picturesque elaboration of the Victorian stage; this involved occasional revival of neglected plays of the period
- two world wars with their attendant horrors made people view the violence of dramatists such as Webster and Ford as a valid comment on the world
- cultural changes of the 1960s – greater sexual openness, abolition of theatre censorship and questioning of accepted values, e.g. Shakespeare's greatness – opened the way for greater experimentation in theatre, including revivals of forgotten Renaissance dramatists

Subsequent popularity

- post 1960s, the play appeals to a new taste for gutsy, visceral drama (cf plays of Mark Ravenhill, Sarah Kane)
- its social/political/religious criticism (give examples) also fits with anti-establishment attitudes and cynicism
- following an explosion of new critical ideologies, we can now see in the play ideas that appeal to our cultural preoccupations, e.g. feminism, social class (give examples)
- we are now prepared to accept writers like Ford as being *different* from Shakespeare, but not necessarily *inferior*

Conclusion

- now that we can see beyond the narrow obsession with incest and the supposed superiority of Shakespeare, we have come to see the many qualities that make this simply a good play (give examples)

Top band marking guidelines

Note: Not all AOs carry equal weight in all specifications.

AO1 Coherent and lucid expression in a well-organised answer. Clear conceptual grasp of the importance of cultural context in literary interpretation.

AO2 Evidence of detailed knowledge and understanding of text and aspects of it that might have affected attitudes to it at different periods. Shows overall grasp of the type of play this is, and can summon specific references/quotations to support points made.

AO3 This AO has little application to this particular essay.

AO4 Demonstrates awareness of a range of different interpretations of play and response to the problems it raises. Articulates confident, independent judgements on possible reasons for changes in attitudes to play, and its varied fortunes on stage.

AO5 Shows genuine understanding of the contexts in which dramatic texts have been read and performed. Confidently evaluates cultural influences in reception of play, particularly in the theatre. Demonstrates knowledge and awareness of historical and sociological changes, and developments in literary and theatrical taste, which have affected reception of play.

 Act IV scene 2 concludes both of the play's subplots. Do you regard this as a strength or a weakness of the play's structure?

Possible ideas to include in a plan

Introduction

- briefly outline what the two subplots are: Bergetto and Hippolita
- briefly consider place of subplots in tragedy; refer to unities
- tackle assumption underlying question: that subplots should be integrated into main plot throughout the play
- suggest that this assumption is not necessarily valid: it depends on the play

What function do the subplots have?

- they establish the inappropriate/unsavoury nature of Annabella's potential marriage partners, making her choice of her brother seem understandable
- they establish the social background of the play and its dubious morality
- the Bergetto plot adds comedy to balance the play's more serious parts
- the Hippolita plot presents us with a contrasting view of the choices available to women and how they respond in a male-dominated world
- Bergetto's and Hippolita's deaths demonstrate the dangers of revenge and how it tends to backfire, as well as the hypocrisy of those who sit in judgement

Explain how both subplots are rounded off in IV.2

- Ford uses Richardetto as the link between the two subplots

- he employs Richardetto economically to forego his own revenge on Soranzo, to moralise on Soranzo's inevitable downfall, to urge Philotis to enter a convent after the death of her fiancé, and to suggest the virtues of a spiritual/religious life

Explain your view of how this affects the structure of the play either successfully or adversely

If you think the structure works well:

- the subplots have served their purpose and can now be dispensed with
- the focus narrows on to the Soranzo/Annabella/Giovanni triangle, which drives forward relentlessly from the very long IV.3
- from now on the dramatic tension never slackens, as play builds to its bloody climax

If you think the structure doesn't work well:

- two important characters who have engaged our interest are suddenly dropped from the play
- the richness of the play's social world is diminished
- losing the comic tone of Bergetto's scenes lessens the play's dramatic variety and makes it too intense

Conclusion

- briefly sum up key points made
- perhaps note that some directors have cut the Bergetto plot; emphasise the challenge for directors and actors in making the play's structure dramatically effective

Top band marking guidelines

Note: Not all AOs carry equal weight in all specifications.

AO1   Coherent and lucid expression in a relevant and well-organised answer. A clear conceptual grasp of the implicit assumptions underlying the question, and of the nature of dramatic construction. Also grasps that this essay demands candidate to come down strongly on one side or the other, rather than presenting a balanced view.

AO2   Evidence of detailed knowledge and accurate understanding of text. Confident grasp of subplots and their functions, and of how IV.2 rounds them off. Supporting evidence and quotations summoned as appropriate. Possibly shows awareness of play as tragedy and how this relates to structural issues.

AO3   Demonstrates implicit and explicit grasp of how writer's chosen structure affects audience response. Understands how subplots might function and how humour, tension, climax, contrast and narrowing of focus might all contribute to desired impact.

AO4   Confidence in offering independent judgement on success of play's structure. Opinions are conceptualised and effectively argued. Refers to judgements of critics/practitioners on effectiveness of subplots/structure.

AO5   Aware of how conceptions of tragedy/the unities have affected concepts of dramatic structure. Shows grasp of audience, not readers, as primary receptors of dramatic text, and able to judge potential audience response to structure. Appreciates how practitioners can help determine audience response when the play is performed.

Sample essays

The two essays that follow are not offered as realistic examples of what an AS/ A-level candidate could actually hope to write in an exam, but to give a sense of how different types of question might be tackled. The first considers the significance of the play's title, and could have been written without having the text available in the exam, though quotations and line references would have been more limited. The second presents a comparison of two speeches, and would definitely have needed the text available for close reference. The same questions could have been tackled in a variety of ways, with considerable change of focus and emphasis from different candidates. Your own knowledge and understanding of the play and its contexts should give you the confidence to write effective essays on any subject the examiners can devise.

Sample essay 1

What significance do you attach to the title of the play?

'Tis Pity She's a Whore is not a title likely to elicit a neutral response; indeed, in times more squeamish than Ford's own it has been found objectionable. A Victorian editor of Ford's plays referred to it as Annabella and Giovanni rather than what he somewhat coyly called 'a much coarser' title, and the potential sponsor of a production at the National Theatre unsuccessfully demanded a less offensive substitute. Yet the title Ford chose carries with it important implications, as well as levels of irony, that it would be a 'pity' to eliminate.

Perhaps the least obvious of the implications of the title is its prioritising of Annabella as the play's central character, separating her from her romantic partner in a way that love tragedies – Romeo and Juliet, Antony and Cleopatra – generally do not do. Ford makes Annabella herself identify her story as 'A wretched, woeful woman's tragedy' (V.1.8), so that Giovanni is marginalised as a merely incidental figure in her drama. In terms of the lines they speak and the time they are on stage, this seems unfair; however, it may perhaps appear more appropriate in view of the differing degree of sympathy the play elicits for the two lovers – a point I shall return to later.

The two key words of the title deserve closer consideration. By conventional moral standards, certainly in Ford's time and even in our own, to classify Annabella as a 'whore' seems entirely reasonable, even though she falls far short of trading her sexual favours for financial gain. For most audiences, until well into the twentieth century, the fact that Annabella indulges in sexual intercourse outside marriage, and with her brother, no less, would be enough to merit the title's offensive noun. To compound her sins, she conceals not merely her incestuous relationship, but also her pregnancy, from the man she then marries, and is utterly unrepentant when the truth is discovered, glorying in her assertion of Soranzo's inferiority to her lover, claiming he is 'not worthy once to name / His name without true worship' (IV.3.40–41). There were almost certainly members of Ford's original audiences who would have agreed with Soranzo's generalisation, motivated by Annabella's behaviour, that it is 'as common / To err in frailty as to be a woman' (IV.3.144–45) – 'frailty' meaning sexual weakness.

Despite this, Annabella is not portrayed unsympathetically. We first see her as the victim of social expectations, and although her father claims he 'would not have her marry wealth, but love' (I.3.11), her three suitors form an unappealing prospect: the violently jealous Grimaldi, the simpleton Bergetto, and the aristocratic Soranzo, with his dubious sexual history. Perhaps it is not surprising that she finds more attractive material closer to home. Though she has clearly loved her brother for some time (see I.2.239–46), he overcomes her moral scruples by a blatant lie, claiming to have the sanction of the 'holy Church' for their love (I.2.236–37), and as for marrying Soranzo, she is urged to this by the Friar, for her 'honour's safety' as much as to 'save [her] soul' (III.6.36–37). Her pregnancy is an unexpected misfortune, her repentance apparently genuine, and she elicits our sympathy, too, in suffering Hippolita's terrifying curse (IV.1.94–97).

The subsequent verbal abuse and physical violence she undergoes from Soranzo further condition our response, and Ford effectively manipulates our moral judgement, as she is murdered by her brother and lover, through her final despairing cry, 'Brother, unkind, unkind' (V.5.93) – the adjective signifying 'unnatural' as much as 'cruel'. Here, the second key word of the title powerfully strikes a chord, as we feel genuine 'pity' for her fate. It is important to realise that 'pity' does not just imply that we feel sorry for her, as in modern English usage. Rather, it reminds us of Aristotle's ideas on tragedy, that it should arouse 'pity and terror' in the audience, with a corresponding purging of our emotions. Annabella's fate certainly arouses such a response, justifying her own perception of her story as a tragedy (see V.1.8). Giovanni's subsequent physical mutilation of her body can only enhance the audience's emotional distress.

In contrast to the pity Ford evokes for Annabella, Giovanni undergoes his trials and meets his destiny largely without our sympathy. He seems unfitted to be a tragic hero, and for much of the time seems selfish, petulant, sullen and manipulative. Though we never question the depth of his feelings for his sister, there is something singularly unattractive about Giovanni, and Annabella is effectively his victim as well as the victim of her own passions and the demands of society. Perhaps she is a 'whore', but Ford does indeed invite our 'pity' for her.

For an audience unfamiliar with the play, its closing lines will come as a surprise. Perhaps, until they are spoken, such spectators will have accepted the title almost without question. When delivered with the outward moral authority of the Cardinal, however, they require a more considered response. This is the man who has singularly failed to dispense justice after the murder of Bergetto, arousing Florio's resentful observation that something is wrong in the world 'When cardinals think murder's not amiss' (III.9.67). Such a man, we feel, is untrustworthy as a moral arbiter on Annabella's behaviour – particularly when we have just seen him cynically confiscate her family's assets 'to the Pope's proper use' (V.6.150). His expression of 'pity' thus seems insincere, and his judgement of Annabella as a 'whore' also becomes an irritatingly unsatisfactory designation, forcing us to redefine Annabella's status for ourselves. As we leave the theatre, the play's title has thus become an object of moral and dramatic scrutiny, rather than a mere tag that we can thoughtlessly accept.

Sample essay 2

Write a comparison of the speeches in which Soranzo and Giovanni express their love for Annabella: Soranzo at II.2.1–18, Giovanni at II.5.45–58.

Of the four men who lay claim to a relationship with Annabella, only two, Giovanni and Soranzo, succeed in possessing her, the first sexually and the second in marriage. Ford draws explicit comparisons between the two rivals, who end up locked in plans of mutual revenge, and in these two speeches their romantic feelings towards Annabella are held up for consideration. There are surprising similarities between the speeches, revealing a closer affinity between the two than we may expect, and both show themselves to be influenced by the ideas embodied in conventional love poetry.

At the opening of II.2, we find Soranzo actually engaged in reading a love poem by Sannazaro, expressing the emotional pain of love. In his infatuation with Annabella, Soranzo disputes Sannazaro's analysis and refashions his lines to convey not love's pains but its pleasures. Only at the end of Soranzo's speech does he turn to consider Annabella's physical attractions, in talking of her 'diviner cheeks'; Giovanni, on the other hand, concentrates entirely on her physical qualities, moving from her face to her sexual organs, which he coyly refrains from naming. Giovanni's praise of Annabella takes the form of a conventional type of love poetry, the blazon, in which the mistress's qualities are catalogued in a series of elaborate similes. One key difference between the two speeches is that Soranzo's is a soliloquy, interrupted ironically by the 'intrusion' of his former mistress, while Giovanni's is delivered to the Friar, as part of an attempt to convince him of the validity of his incest, contrasting with his mentor's moral revulsion.

In rewriting the two lines of Sannazaro's that he quotes, Soranzo replaces the poet's vision of love's 'pain', 'unrest' and 'disdain' with an alternative one of its sweetness, 'pleasures' and 'joys', claiming that 'Love's measure' – metaphorically its dance or its rhythm – is not 'extreme' but moderate ('the mean'). Ironically, Soranzo's subsequent experience with Annabella confirms Sannazaro's analysis rather than his own, with moderation soon giving way to extremity of passion and violence. It is interesting, though, that even in Soranzo's romanticised view, love is an essentially painful experience; he talks of the 'oppression' laid on his 'bosom', and of being beaten with a rod. However, being in love is all about worshipping the very thing that is hurting you – 'kiss[ing] the rod that made the smart' and finding love's 'annoys' sweet. Also notable is that Soranzo's reflections are as much about his disagreement with the 'smooth licentious poet' as they are about his love for Annabella: Sannazaro's name is mentioned three times, as well as his highly regarded poem about Venice, which had 'gained him such a sum of gold'. All of this serves to distance Soranzo from any genuine depth of feeling, as we see him engaged in an essentially intellectual exercise.

There is artificiality, too, in Giovanni's praise of Annabella, which works, as the form of the blazon invariably did, through a catalogue of comparisons. Her face is a 'world of variety', consisting of the 'colour', 'perfumes', 'jewels', golden 'threads', 'flowers' and 'music' of her lips, breath, eyes, hair, cheeks and voice. The rest of her bodily qualities are omitted except for her private parts, perhaps indicating where Giovanni's real interest lies. In describing them coyly as 'what is […] for pleasure framed', Giovanni is ostensibly sensitive to the Friar's moral prudery, but perhaps also subconsciously conveying his own sense of shame. While Soranzo's speech is essentially a debate with the poet Sannazaro, Giovanni's has a more compelling motivation in his need to persuade the Friar of the validity of his love for Annabella. He reassures the Friar that, if he hears Annabella's confession, he will realise that she reciprocates Giovanni's love, and his aim is to elicit his mentor's 'pity' that the two of them 'Should have been sundered from each other's arms'. The Friar's response does indeed express 'pity', but not for the reasons Giovanni would prefer.

The form and structure of the verse in which the two lovers express their feelings reflect the contrast in the nature of their speeches. Soranzo's speech is built around the two lines he quotes from Sannazaro and his own rewriting of them. The status of these lines as 'poetry' is emphasised by their smooth rhythms and their rhyming couplets, making them stand out from the less regular, more broken quality of Soranzo's intervening comments, where the use of colloquial elisions and caesura to separate the brief phrases – 'What's here? Look't o'er again. 'Tis so' – emphasises the active working of his mind. Having crafted his own alternative couplet, however, Soranzo's verse acquires greater fluency, building from line 12 into a long, six-line sentence celebrating Annabella as an object of inspiration. The sense of the speaker being swiftly carried away to the inevitable climax of his lover's 'diviner cheeks' is created through the sequence of run-on lines, with barely a pause for breath. This makes Vasques's interruption all the more effective.

Giovanni's speech begins conversationally as he addresses the Friar, changing tone as he becomes preoccupied with Annabella's attractions. Again, the verse is regular, though divided into self-contained comparative phrases which could be used to give it a more hesitant air, as if the speaker were coining each image spontaneously. The concluding rhyming couplet, which should produce a climactic effect, is undermined by its coy avoidance of explicit reference to Annabella's private parts, allegedly to spare the Friar's blushes. The effect of bathos is something that an actor could emphasise either to create humour or to suggest Giovanni's uncharacteristic sense of shame.

In making both Soranzo and Giovanni responsive to forms of love poetry, Ford is perhaps suggesting something rather old-fashioned about them both, fitting in with other elements of the play that place it in the recent past. Sannazaro was writing in the late fifteenth and early sixteenth centuries, while the blazon was a characteristic form of Elizabethan love poetry, often expressed in sonnet form – of which Giovanni's final couplet is reminiscent. Shakespeare had effectively deconstructed the artificiality of such catalogues of comparisons in his Sonnet 130, 'My mistress' eyes are nothing like the sun'. Perhaps, then, to an audience of around 1630, both Giovanni's and Soranzo's expressions of love may have seemed somewhat hollow and superficial.

Further study

Editions of the play

All good editions of *'Tis Pity She's a Whore* contain useful notes and stimulating introductions. Some of the best are listed below:

Barker, S. (ed.) (1997) Routledge English Texts, Routledge.

Bawcutt, N. W. (ed.) (1966) Regents Renaissance Drama, Arnold.

Roper, D. (ed.) (1975) Revels Plays, Methuen.

Roper, D. (ed.) (1997) Revels Student Editions, Manchester University Press.

Wiggins, M. (ed.) (2003) New Mermaids, 2nd edn, A. and C. Black. This is the edition that has been used for the textual references in this Student Text Guide.

Criticism of the play and Ford's works in general

Anderson, D. K., Jr (1972) *John Ford*, Twayne.

Anderson, D. K., Jr (ed.) (1986) *'Concord in Discord': The Plays of John Ford, 1586–1986*, AMS Press.

Brooke, N. (1979) *Horrid Laughter in Jacobean Tragedy*, Barnes and Noble. Contains a chapter on *'Tis Pity*.

Hopkins, L. (1994) *John Ford's Political Theatre*, Manchester University Press.

Leech, C. (1957) *John Ford and the Drama of his Time*, Chatto and Windus.

Neill, M. (ed.) (1988) *John Ford: Critical Re-Visions*, Cambridge University Press.

Scott, M. (1982) *Renaissance Drama and a Modern Audience*, Macmillan. Contains a chapter on *'Tis Pity*.

Simkin, S. (ed.) (2001) *Revenge Tragedy*, New Casebooks, Palgrave.

White, M. (1998) *Renaissance Drama in Action*, Routledge. This contains an interesting case study on the original staging of *'Tis Pity* (pp. 156–76).

Wymer, R. (1995) *Webster and Ford*, Macmillan.

Context

Gurr, A. (1992) *The Shakespearean Stage 1574–1642*, 3rd edn, Cambridge University Press.

Sanders, J. (1999) *Caroline Drama*, Writers and their Work, Northcote House.

Wiggins, M. (2000) *Shakespeare and the Drama of his Time*, Oxford University Press.

Audiovisual resources and the internet

'Tis Pity She's a Whore has been adapted for film, directed by Giuseppe Patroni Griffi in 1973, with Charlotte Rampling as Annabella and Oliver Tobias as Giovanni; and for BBC television, directed by Roland Joffé in 1980, with Cherie Lunghi as Annabella and Kenneth Cranham as Giovanni. Neither of these adaptations is readily available, but it may be possible to track down copies in specialist libraries and archives.

Searching for 'John Ford' on the internet is likely to offer more hits relating to the famous Hollywood film director than the Caroline dramatist; the title of the play itself will probably yield richer returns, but be careful to avoid the chance of eliciting pornography. The most reliable site is probably the following, though it may prove limited in what it has to offer to AS or A-level students: **www.luminarium.org/sevenlit/ford/index.html**

A number of Shakespeare websites contain material on Shakespeare's contemporaries, and theatre websites are likely to have details of current or previous productions of the play. The following may be useful:

- **www.rsc.org.uk** is the Royal Shakespeare Company's website.
- **www.shakespeares-globe.org** is the official website of the reconstructed Globe Theatre. There are various links that should direct you to information on the indoor theatres of Shakespeare's time, which would be more relevant to Ford's play.
- **www.shakespeare.org.uk** is the website for the Shakespeare Birthplace Trust. From there you can access the Shakespeare Centre Library in Stratford-upon-Avon. This houses the archives of the Royal Shakespeare Company, where you can look up the records of its two productions of *'Tis Pity* (1977 and 1991), including promptbooks, programmes, photographs and reviews. Individual students and small groups can arrange to watch the archive video of David Leveaux's 1991 production. Although recorded in performance with a fixed camera, this is nevertheless worth seeing. Find out more on the website, via the 'Library & Archives' link.
- **www.nationaltheatre.org.uk** is the National Theatre's website, through which you can find out how to access records of its 1972 and 1988 productions of the play. Enter 'archive' in the 'SearchNT' box.